D1582871

In Defence
of the
Imagination

IN DEFENCE
OF THE
IMAGINATION

*The Charles Eliot Norton
Lectures 1979–1980*

HELEN GARDNER

CLARENDON PRESS · OXFORD
1982

Oxford University Press, Walton Street, Oxford OX2 6DP
London Glasgow New York Toronto
Delhi Bombay Calcutta Madras Karachi
Kuala Lumpur Singapore Hong Kong Tokyo
Nairobi Dar es Salaam Cape Town
Melbourne Wellington
and associate companies in
Beirut Berlin Ibadan Mexico City

Published in the United States by
Oxford University Press, New York

British Library Cataloguing in Publication Data
Gardner, Helen
    In defence of the imagination.
    1. English prose literature—History and criticism.
    I. Title
    828'.08 PR753
    ISBN 0-19-812639-5

Filmset in 'Monophoto' Plantin by Eta Services (Typesetters) Ltd.,
Beccles, Suffolk, England
and printed in the United States of America

Preface

With some revision and expansion these are the lectures I gave at Harvard as Charles Eliot Norton Professor of Poetry during the session 1979–80. I have added to them, as an appendix, a lecture upon a related topic that I gave in London while I was back in England for a break at Christmas.

The honour of being invited to give the Norton Lectures is accompanied by the pleasure of being invited to spend some six months at Harvard as a member of the University, where I was welcomed by old friends, such as Douglas and Hazel Bush, Gwynne and Betty Evans, Harry and Elena Levin, and Jeremy and Janey Knowles, and made many new friends. Among them, I must particularly thank Professor Jerome Buckley, who was responsible for making arrangements for the lectures but far exceeded his duties by making each lecture the prelude to a celebration, and Professor David Perkins, who made my life very easy by finding a graduate student, Mark MacPherson, to fetch and carry for me. I could not have had a more kind and assiduous attendant and chauffeur. I have to thank Professor and Mrs Frazier, co-masters of Currier House, for giving me the privileges of a fellow and providing me with a guest-flat in the House, as well as for some delightful festive occasions arranged in my honour. I greatly enjoyed the day-to-day contact with students in Currier House, and the opportunity for informal conversation with young people of widely differing backgrounds, experience, and interests. In addition to giving the six public lectures, I shared a course with Professor Ronald Bush on Pound, Eliot, and Joyce, and have to thank him for much helpfulness in initiating me into the ways of a strange university, as well as for conversations on Eliot, and a trip to Gloucester. During my second semester I conducted a graduate seminar on Donne, which was a very happy experience, the class being keen and hard-working, and very

v

tolerant of what must have seemed to them a rather unorthodox way of taking a seminar.

I am much indebted to conversations with Harriett Hawkins, Elsie Duncan-Jones, Katherine Duncan-Jones, and Andrew Wilson during the time I was planning and reading for my lectures. At Harvard I had the pleasure and privilege of conversation with Professor Amos Wilder, and have corresponded with him since my return. I am grateful to the late Morris Weitz of Brandeis University for encouraging me to take as my subject recent developments in literary criticism, and for his friendship.

I have to thank Mrs Valerie Eliot for permission to quote from critical essays by T. S. Eliot, and Mrs Diana Trilling for permission to quote from essays by Lionel Trilling; Faber and Faber Ltd. and Random House, Inc., for permission to quote lines from 'In Memory of W. B. Yeats' (from *Collected Poems of W. H. Auden*) and from 'September 1, 1939' (from *The English Auden: Poems, Essays and Dramatic Writings 1927–1939 by W. H. Auden*); Davis Poynter Ltd. for permission to quote the poem 'Satie at the End of Term' from *On the Apthorpe Road and Other Poems* (1975) by Simon Curtis; the Council of the Modern Humanities Research Association and the editors of *The Modern Language Review* for permission to reprint 'Literary Biography'.

If this volume bore a dedication it would be to the memory of T. S. Eliot, who was constantly in my mind as I wrote my lectures and during the time I spent in his own university, Harvard:

> the communication
> Of the dead is tongued with fire beyond the language
> of the living.

HELEN GARDNER

Contents

Chapter I

Present Discontents

When I received the invitation to come to Harvard as the Charles Eliot Norton Professor of Poetry, I was deeply conscious of the honour paid me but apprehensive. I was afraid I had nothing new or original to say. But as I hesitated before replying, I remembered what had been one of the great experiences of my first year at Oxford. Twice a week I cycled up the High in winter evenings over Magdalen Bridge, looking up as I passed at Magdalen Tower, changing according to the light and the variable weather but subsisting the same through change, to hear Gilbert Murray lecture to a crowded audience in the North School of the Examination Schools. He was giving at Oxford the lectures he had given at Harvard as the first Charles Eliot Norton Professor of Poetry. I can still see in my mind's eye Murray's extraordinarily noble face and hear in memory his beautiful voice as, with a kind of quiet fervour and a deep conviction, he spoke of the classical tradition in poetry, feeling, as he wrote in his preface, that 'amid the whirl of new doctrines and old misunderstandings about art and poetry, there was a need for a restatement of the "classical" view'.[1] I was also consoled by remembering that Samuel Johnson, whom Eliot in his Norton lectures praised as 'a type of critical integrity', declared that 'it is not sufficiently considered, that men more frequently require to be reminded than informed'.[2] It seemed likely that those who had invited me had not expected that, at the stage of life I had reached, I was likely to have received some new revelation of the significance of literature to make me call in question the assumptions I had lived by and tested in fifty years of teaching and writing, and that my best response to the invitation would be to attempt a restatement of the humanist belief in the value of a study of literature as the core of a liberal education in the 'whirl of new doctrines' today.

I am perhaps particularly suited to this enterprise, since what to most people concerned with literature has been a movement whose growth they have watched has been something I became fully conscious of only when it was full grown, widely established, and flourishing like a green bay tree. I refer to the newest form of 'new criticism', transplanted into England and America from France. For around ten years, from the middle sixties until three or four years ago, I was working largely at home, occupied in putting together a large anthology and with an intensive study of manuscript material, largely in photo-copies, with occasional trips to Cambridge to check against the originals. I was also much burdened with professorial duties and the usual load of committees. For much of the time I had difficulty in getting about and using libraries. So I fell behind in my reading of new critical works, except those dealing with Donne or Eliot, and in my reading in periodicals. It was, therefore, with surprise and a sense of shock that, being relieved of professorial duties, having sent my book to the press, being able to move about freely again, and being anxious to bring myself up-to-date, I found myself a kind of literary Rip Van Winkle in a strange, disturbing world. To begin with I met an extraordinary new vocabulary, or rather many strange and new vocabularies, according to what other disciplines—linguistics, psychology, philosophy, theology—the critic thought provided him with a model or a method. Beyond these technical terms, which could often be found in the Supplement to the Oxford Dictionary (as long as the word did not begin with a letter after N), there were other strange words, loosely derived from Greek or from Latin, both classical and medieval, coinages whose meaning could be puzzled out by recourse to classical dictionaries. And further, there were words which the critic had made up for his own pleasure in a mood of high spirits or 'playfulness', a word which for some appeared to be a synonym for critical activity.

More disturbing than this wilful and self-indulgent use of language was the dismissal of the author as the creator of the work and the denial of objective status to the text. The

author gave place to the reader, on the ground that the text
has no existence as 'an object exterior to the psyche and
history of the man who interprets it'.[3] Since the reader may
be any and every reader from now to the end of time, texts
were to be regarded as susceptible of an infinite number of
meanings, and, since no criteria were proposed by which
any meaning could be rejected or accepted, were in fact
meaningless. The critic, therefore, regarding it as
impossible to fulfil what has always been regarded as his
prime duty—to illuminate the author's meaning, now
declared to be totally irrecoverable—created meanings
within the void (*le vide*) of the text, or, to put it another
way, imported meanings into a text that had no determinate
meaning of its own. Milton, it appeared, was totally deluded
when he wrote that books 'do contain a potency of life in
them to be as active as that soul whose progeny they are;
nay, they do preserve as in a vial the purest efficacy and
extraction of that living intellect that bred them'. On the
contrary, properly regarded, they are 'absolutely dead
things'. Persons, like myself, who had thought when
reading a poem that through the medium of the printed
page a man, although long dead, was speaking to them, are
misguided. We had not learnt how to distinguish between
parole and *écriture*, speech, which we hear, and writing,
which we read. A written text is merely black marks on a
white ground, emitting an infinite play of significances in
which the critic may sport like a dolphin. He is the real
artist, responding to this play of significances, liberated
from 'the obligation to be right (a standard that simply
drops out)' and concerned only to be 'interesting (a
standard that can be met without any reference at all to an
illusory objectivity)'. The critic from whom I am quoting,
Stanley Fish, goes on: 'Rather than restoring or recovering
texts, I am in the business of making texts and of teaching
others to make them by adding to their repertoire of
strategies.'[4] This makes the study of literature sound like a
highly sophisticated war-game with the object of
annihilating the author on the field of battle of the text.
Hostility to the authority of the author as creator of the text
was expressed by other terms: Deconstruction, which

makes it the critic's duty to unmake what the poet, or maker, has made, and Antithetical Reading, which, applying the insights of the latest psychological sage, finds in the poem the opposite of the meaning that the 'naive reader' finds and that he has assumed the author intended him to find. Words such as these, and negating verbs such as 'de-idealize', 'de-mystify' and 'de-normalize' used to describe critical activity, suggest an underlying destructive urge, like that of a child who with glee knocks down a pile of bricks which his playmate has with great pains built up into a house.

Similar tendencies appeared among some of the critics who attempted what used to be called 'interpretation', that is, who considered the import of the work as a whole rather than the play of significances emitted by single words and phrases. This activity was now being given the more impressive name of 'hermeneutics', a term adopted from Biblical criticism via Heidegger. The earliest use of this term in the criticism of secular literature to be recorded in the Oxford Supplement is from the *Listener* in 1965, but I have found it employed by Elder Olson in America the year before, and Eliot used it, though I think ironically, in 1956. It has now become widely fashionable, and a false notion of the primacy of the 'spiritual senses' of Scripture over the literal sense, now, to make clear its degradation, called the 'carnal sense', has been used to justify treating the literal sense as something to be resisted or ignored in favour of the secret senses uncovered by the critic. This has gone along with a revival of interest in Gnosticism. Even when the myths of what has been described as that 'sombre and repellent theosophy'[5] are not explicitly referred to, the rejection of determinate meanings in texts reflects, and is by some tied to, the idea that the world of our daily experience, mediated to us through the reports of our senses, is meaningless, indeterminate, and unpredictable. Such a notion has obvious affinities with the Gnostic rejection of the material universe as not the creation of the Supreme God, but as having resulted from some Fall, whether by mischance or evil will, among the aeons or emanations of the Deity. And the barrier set up between the ordinary reader and the expert in hermeneutics parallels the Gnostic distinction between the fleshly majority of mankind and the few 'spiritual' men, or *illuminati* who are capable of *gnosis* or illumination.

This rapid and impressionistic account of the newest kind of new criticism, inspired by the *nouvelle critique*, is unfair without my acknowledging that many of the critics who have adopted procedures based on the rejection of the objective existence of the text are learned and widely read and, in many cases, have in the past made substantial contributions to knowledge. The intellectual liveliness and energy displayed by the more distinguished of them is impressive. I would not wish to say that I have received no incidental benefits from my reading of them, from occasional subtle insights; and I do not wish to reject the possibility that their work may have genuine interest for psychologists and for philosophers interested in problems of language. But I am neither a psychologist nor, alas, a philosopher. I am a student of literature. And for me, the overwhelming impression gained is of frivolity and triviality. The new New Criticism has no connection with my own experience of reading or with the values I have found in that experience.

I do not wish to spend much time on the axioms from which these new procedures arise. They exaggerate partial truisms into patent falsities and elevate difficulties into impossibilities. Nobody has ever denied that our responses to works of art are individual and necessarily subjective, and that, in one sense, and a very important one, they have a peculiar meaning for each one of us. But this fact does not prevent our discussing them with others upon the basis of a shared recognition of their existence and particularity as objects, and disciplining our purely personal responses to arrive at a common judgement, finding our responses enriched in the process. A book we have not read is no more non-existent than a country which we have not visited. We may know quite a lot about it as an object, just as we can know quite a lot about a country we have not visited by what we have been told and what we have read. Most people, travelling for pleasure and not for business, go to places and countries because of what they have read or been told. This has made them want to go and see for themselves. Similarly, information about a book and its author can excite in us a desire to read it. We all know there is a world of difference between acquiring information about a book and experiencing a book in our reading of it, as there is between reading about a country and actually visiting it, or better still living in it for a while. The distinction between knowing about a poem and knowing a poem itself was the basis of the old New Criticism's revolt against what seemed to its proponents an overconcentration among academics on information, to the neglect of the actual experience of reading. But they concentrated on interpretation and explication of texts as a means of making other readers better readers, as a contribution towards the common pursuit of a truer and fuller understanding. It was possible and fruitful to argue against their readings. As an example, I might refer to Humphry House's generous and courteous examination, in his Clark Lectures on Coleridge, of Robert Penn Warren's interpretation of *The Ancient Mariner*, a model of close critical interpretation.[6] Again, nobody would claim that it is possible to be absolutely right, declare the absolute truth, or say the last word about anything so complex as even a short lyric, much less an epic poem or a long novel. But this does not mean that we cannot distinguish between true and false statements and right and wrong judgements, and that we should not aim at being right and accept correction when we have been shown to be wrong, and have the grace to be pleased that our error has led to the establishment of a truth.

Again, it is of course perfectly true that the author is not present in the flesh, as we read his book, for us to interrogate him. Even if he were, interrogation might not yield any very satisfying results. Authors, in my experience, do not take very kindly to being asked what they meant, and very often reply that they meant what they said. But to extend these truisms to deny that we are conscious as we read a book or a poem that we are reading the expression of an individual mind and sensibility, and that this is conveyed to us by an individual manner of expression that, like a voice, belongs to one person, would only be sense if we were prepared to deny the possibility of any communication of mind with mind by the medium of the written word: to deny that, as Donne wrote, letters as much as conversation can 'mingle souls'. Further, although at any moment we are reading a single work, that work is usually part of an *œuvre*, which we either know in part or can get to know. As we read more and more of an author's work we come to know a way of regarding the world of human experience, a mode of expression, and an individual idiom that is characteristic of all his works however various they may be. And the more we become familiar with his writings, the more we enjoy the particularities of single works. I suppose we have all had the experience of having been so excited by a book or a poem by an author we had not read before that for a while we wanted to read nothing else but books or poems by the same author, and then to re-read them. It is ironic that the rejection by this new school of criticism of the author's authority has coincided with a proliferation of literary biographies, and their wide popularity, and with the great interest taken in seeing authors at work: in tracing the process, through drafts and rewritings, by which a writer wrestles with words and meanings to arrive at the final artefact. Both the biography of a writer and the study of him in his workshop require to be used with delicacy and tact when we come to discuss the work made; yet both enable us to see that work as a historical object, made by an individual man, who lived in a certain place at a certain time, and made choices and decisions in the making of his work. So my concern remains with authors and their works. Compared with the fruitful enlargement of the capacity to see and think and know and feel, that the experience of reading gives to those who will make the imaginative and intellectual effort to attempt to apprehend the work as its author made it, the sport of 'making texts' and 'importing meanings' is a perverse and barren exercise in ingenuity, a *reductio ad absurdum* of the emphasis which the old New Criticism gave to the importance of the reader's response.

In speaking of this new school of criticism I have brought together critics who are widely different in the use they

make of the ideas of the French theorists. In the same way
'New Criticism' was a term employed to include a great
variety of critics who yet had certain things in common.
The most distinctive of these were the primacy given to
interpretation, to the comparative neglect of evaluation, the
stress on a poem as an embodiment of feelings, emotions,
moods, to the neglect of the cognitive element in poetry,
and a lack of interest in the techniques of poetry, in verse
forms, and poetic devices. New Critics concentrated on
underlying themes and structures at the expense of what
makes a poem a work of deliberate art and gives delight.
They neglected the surface to concentrate on the symbol. A
characteristic of the methods of interpretation used was the
dominance of theories about the nature of literature, and
particularly about the nature of poetry. Some accepted the
Freudian concept of the unconscious, and by it discovered
the latent or inner meaning of works of imagination; others,
following Jung, reduced poems to expressions of a limited
number of myths and archetypes. More often the dominating axioms were the invention of the critic, attempting to
distinguish the language of poetry and literature generally
from the language of science, or declaring that the characteristic language of poetry was 'paradox' or 'irony', or that
the essential language of poetry as distinct from prose was
'ambiguity' or 'plurisignation': that is, multiple verbal
meanings.[7] As hostility between critics and scholars abated,
New Criticism took on a historical dimension. Poems
became the expressions of what was declared to be the
dominant ideology of the period, or of some strand in contemporary thought which the scholar's researches had
discovered and elucidated and which he found to be the
true meaning of the poem. The timeless reader was thus by
some replaced by the original readers or 'the audience', who
became guides to the true interpretation of the author's
mind and his work. This corrected the responses of the
modern reader, who had now to learn to think 'like an
Elizabethan', or to acquire that wonderful abstraction from
reality 'the medieval mind'.

The problems with which the New Critics were
concerned were genuine problems, and reading their works

gave and still gives pleasure and incidental rewards. Many of the leading members of the school were themselves distinguished poets, and all wrote out of a passionate engagement with poetry and a belief in its power to communicate a true vision of reality. Their virtues as well as their limitations were linked with the triumph of the modernist movement, which came to full flower in the year 1922, with the publication of *The Waste Land* and *Ulysses*. The same year saw the publication of I. A. Richards's first book, *The Foundations of Aesthetics*. Two years before the appearance of *The Waste Land*, Eliot had collected the most important of the periodical essays he had been writing between 1917 and 1920 under the title of *The Sacred Wood*, and throughout the twenties he was writing the essays in which he redrew the old accepted map of English literature. Richards followed up his first book with *Principles of Literary Criticism* in 1924, and *Practical Criticism* in 1929. His brilliant pupil, William Empson, began the hunt for multiple meanings in *Seven Types of Ambiguity* in 1930. He took up and extended a method of analysis begun by Robert Graves and Laura Riding. In *A Survey of Modernist Poetry* in 1927 they analysed a Shakespeare sonnet, as printed in the quarto text, against a poem by E. E. Cummings, to show that Shakespeare, read in what they naïvely considered to be his original text, was more difficult than Cummings, difficulty being the criterion of merit. In 1930 also, Wilson Knight produced *The Wheel of Fire*, with an introduction by Eliot, and began the interpretation of Shakespeare by themes and recurrent imagery, which came to be known as 'spatial criticism'. These were the seminal works from which the New Criticism developed in America in the late thirties and forties. A little later a mode of criticism which had begun as a way of reading poetry better was extended to the interpretation of novels.

The years of *entre deux guerres* began with the post-war disillusion, the sense of myriads of lives sacrificed for a 'botched civilisation', an enormous waste, to which Pound gave direct expression in *Mauberley*, and with the desolation of a ruined Europe which its first readers found embodied in *The Waste Land*. Constant economic crises culminated in the world-wide Great Depression, and were accompanied by political instability, which, after Hitler's rise to power, brought the threat, which turned into the certainty, of a second world war. To the historian it is a gloomy period in which it seemed as if Europe had lost the power to renew itself, to find solutions for its economic plight and its political disarray. It was, at the same time, one of the great creative periods in all the arts as it was in science, an age of giants. It remains in my memory as exciting and thrilling as well as deeply distressing and painful. Both the English writers of the twenties (if we may include Pound and Eliot as English by settlement), and the New Critics of America, who developed and systematized Richards's emphasis on 'practical criticism' and Eliot's revision of literary history, realized that they were living in such a period and felt all the excitement and elation that accompanies revolutions of every kind. Like all revolutions, it had appealed back from an immediate, and what was seen as a discredited, past to a true tradition which it declared had been revived. The criticism had a double objective: to commend the writers of the modern movement by creating a climate of opinion in which their works would be received and understood, and to establish them in the true tradition of English poetry. Interpretation played so large a part in their enterprise in order to meet the common complaint that the works of the new masters were difficult to the point of incomprehensibility. The poetry of Pound and Eliot, and Joyce's huge novel, seemed to cry out for it. So methods of criticism were developed that assumed as axiomatic that true poetry was complex and difficult, paradoxical and dense with verbal ambiguities, and that its vessel of communication was the symbolic image in which thought and feeling were fused. Accepting Eliot's theory that in the late seventeenth century 'a dissociation of sensibility set in, from which we have never recovered', they found in Shakespeare and the dramatists who were his contemporaries and followers, and in Donne and his 'school', by a process one scholar described as 'kidnapping Donne', the qualities of 'true poetry'. Thus Donne was justified as being 'modern' by comparison with Eliot, and

Eliot as being in the 'true tradition' by his likeness to Donne.

Eliot himself, who perhaps endured rather more than his fair share of 'interpretation', never regarded interpretation as a legitimate critical activity. In an early essay on 'The Function of Criticism', published in *The Criterion* in 1923,[8] he defined the end of criticism as 'the elucidation of works of art and the correction of taste'. He made clear what he meant by elucidation when he came to speak of 'interpretation', putting the word in inverted commas. It is, he declared, 'only legitimate when it is not interpretation at all, but merely putting the reader in possession of facts which he would otherwise have missed'. He was drawing on his own experience as a University Extension lecturer for the universities of London and Oxford. Eliot did not believe in 'creative criticism'. He saw the work of art as autotelic, but he saw criticism as having an end beyond itself. The critic's role was comparable to the teacher's. His duty is to be useful, and 'to justify his existence' he 'should endeavour to discipline his personal prejudices and cranks . . . and compose his differences with as many of his fellows as possible, in the common pursuit of true judgement'. More than thirty years later, in his lecture on 'The Frontiers of Criticism', given in 1956,[9] he returned to the subject in a tone of polite irony. He reported that he had been sent a volume entitled *Interpretations* in which twelve of the younger English critics had each chosen a well-known poem for analysis. 'The method', Eliot kindly explained, as if we were not all well acquainted with it by 1956, 'is to take a well-known poem . . . without reference to the author or to his other work, analyse it stanza by stanza and line by line, and extract, squeeze, tease, press every drop of meaning out of it that one can. It might be called the lemon-squeezer school of criticism.' Eliot was polite about having found the volume interesting, although he owned he had found reading it 'a very tiring way of passing the time'. But he added that he would have liked, as a test, to see the method applied to a good poem which he did *not* know, because he would have liked to find out whether, after perusing the analysis, he would be able to enjoy the poem. He had found that, after reading the analysis of a poem that he already knew, he had been slow to recover his previous feeling about it. 'It was as if someone had taken a machine to pieces and left me with the task of reassembling the parts.' He went on to refer to his previous definition of the function of criticism as sounding 'somewhat pompous to our ears in 1956', and reworded it to say that it is the function of criticism to 'promote the understanding and the enjoyment of literature', adding 'there is implied here also the negative task of pointing out what should *not* be enjoyed'. He explained that he did not 'think of *enjoyment* and *understanding* as distinct activities—one emotional and the other intellectual', and that by *understanding* he did not mean *explanation*, 'though explanation of what can be explained may often be a necessary preliminary to understanding'. And he went on: 'To understand a poem comes to the same thing as to enjoy it for the right reasons. One might say it means getting from a poem such enjoyment as it is capable of giving: to enjoy a poem under a misunderstanding as to what it is, is to enjoy what is merely a projection of our own mind.' He ended his lecture with a courteous gesture with his right hand, followed by a characteristic qualification with his left, and a query: 'These last thirty years have been, I think, a brilliant period in literary criticism in both Britain and America. It may even come to seem in retrospect, too brilliant. Who knows?'

What was the modern movement in English and American literature has now passed into history. We have to call it the 'modernist movement'. Its great figures—Yeats, Pound, Eliot, Joyce, Lawrence, Wallace Stevens—are now well entrenched in academic syllabuses. The vultures and the crows have moved in over the old battlefields. Writers who once aroused a passionate enthusiasm and as passionate a disapproval are now the prey of bibliographers and textual critics, biographers and editors of letters, and graduate students seeking doctorates. In England the movement came to an abrupt end with the ending of the war and with the appearance of a new generation of poets who came to be dubbed the 'Movement' when their works were collected together in 1956 in *New Lines*. The most distinguished of them, Philip Larkin, looked to Hardy as his model and among his older contemporaries to John Betjeman. Donald Davie, who provided a theoretical and historical justification for the 'Movement', was an academic, a critic, and scholar as well as a poet. So, for a while, were John Wain and Kingsley Amis, who are novelists as well as poets; but they abandoned the security of the groves of academe to make their living by writing. Davie's two books, published in the fifties, *Purity of Diction in English Verse* and *Articulate Energy*, argued strongly that poets should respect the common meaning of words and not employ a private and personal language, and that the inherited systems of syntax were man's prime instrument of articulation. The abandonment of syntax by modernist poets showed, he argued, a failure of poetic nerve, a loss of faith in the ability of the conscious mind to order its experience. The attack was mainly against Eliot. The mood of the fifties was summed up by Graham Hough in *Image and Experience* (1960). He declared that the whole modernist enterprise in England had been a cul-de-sac. Although it had produced some great art, it was a blind alley. In the twentieth century the true tradition of English poetry was represented by Hardy, Robert Graves, Edwin Muir, John Betjeman, and Philip Larkin. In the same decade Frank Kermode, in *The Romantic Image* (1957), demolished Eliot's theory of the catastrophic dissociation of sensibility in the mid-seventeenth century. Donne was seen again as the 'Monarch of Wit' (the title of Blair Leishman's study in 1951), and Milton, far from having been dislodged, was very much still there and very much alive.

The difficulty of accepting *tout court* Hough's dismissal of the modernist poets as having gone off the beaten track, or highway, and down a cul-de-sac lies in his concession that all the same they produced great art. The poets he lists, from Hardy to Larkin, as having written in the true tradition, although good and serious poets in different ways, cannot by any standard of evaluation be called great. They give much delight but it is a limited delight. They do not astonish or very greatly extend the experience and the imagination of their readers. Some years ago, in the early sixties, I was reading through some recent volumes that had been submitted for the Queen's Prize for Poetry. I had a young poet staying with me—I hope I need hardly add that he was not a competitor—and I sent him up to bed with a batch of these. At breakfast next morning I asked him what he thought of them and he said, 'They are terribly unambitious, aren't they?' Nobody could possibly make such a comment on Yeats, continually remaking himself into his old age; on Eliot, who was also an explorer, never finding a style to rest in; on Pound embarking on the epic scheme of the *Cantos,* taking it up again—'As a lone ant from a broken ant-hill / from the wreckage of Europe'—to write *The Pisan Cantos,* and then still undefeated going on from them into his final silence; or, to turn to the novel, on Joyce, not content with *Ulysses,* in poverty and near-blindness undertaking *Finnegans Wake.* With the exception of Ted Hughes, who has a violent and disturbing imagination, a command of free rhythms, and of metaphor and image, that separate him from the poets of the Movement, post-war English poetry has not been exciting. The American poets of the post-war period were much more experimental and adventurous than the English; but neither the Beat Poets of San Francisco, nor the Black Mountain Group, nor the confessional and autobiographical poets that followed, could be said to have produced great art. By the mid-sixties the whole conception of great art or high culture was under attack, more vehemently in America than in England. In the interests of total self-expression and of social and sexual liberation, with the aid of various perversions of Freud's teaching, and a Marxism that would have shocked Karl Marx, the inheritance of the past was declared to be irrelevant to modern youth. The natural process of growing up, by which the young of the human species, like animals and birds, leave the parental lair or nest and grow away from their parents, which all societies and civilizations have disciplined by commanding that the young should honour their fathers and mothers, was exaggerated into a generation gap that was treated as impassable, and into a breakdown of communication expressed in the notion of a separate 'youth culture' or 'anti-culture'. Various sages, by immersion in some kind of Medea's cauldron, were able to leap the generation gap and articulate the revolt of the young. This tidal wave has now subsided, although it has left behind it a great deal of human wreckage on the beaches. Most important from the point of view of these lectures was an attack on literary standards and literary values as being élitist, in the interests of the democratization of culture. This notion still burdens some consciences, causing acceptance of debasements of language, and discomfort at applying standards of excellence to works by persons thought to be underprivileged. This is a painful expression of an inverted snobbery and self-consciousness. If, by some wonderful chance, a new Lincoln arose, one wonders whether he would have the courage to defy the image-makers and the public-relations men, and speak with the unselfconscious nobility of the Gettysburg address, a nobility that assumed, or took for granted, that all men are equal, not to be patronized, or talked down to.

There is truth in what Graham Hough said if we rephrase his denigratory dismissal, and regard the modernist movement in poetry as not a blind alley or cul-de-sac, but as the culmination of a tradition which it was impossible to carry further. Eliot in his 1956 lecture, speaking of *Finnegans Wake* 'neither in praise or dispraise of a book which is certainly in the category of works that can be called *monumental*', said of it: 'One book like this is enough.' One might say the same of *The Waste Land*. It has had no progeny at any rate. The quatrain poems, which most writers on Eliot regard as a regrettable deviation from his true path—a view which I do not share—can be felt behind many poems of the twenties and thirties. *The Waste Land*, in spite of all the admiration it has received and still receives—and many regard it as Eliot's masterpiece—has not been a source of poetic energy in the fifty odd years since it appeared. I can think of no later poem that could be seen as an attempt to wrestle with it as a precursor, to use the terminology of an influential modern critic. Frank Kermode said something similar about Wallace Stevens: 'He is a poet who provides a unique, perhaps un-repeatable, solution to the image-and-discourse problem, by making the problem itself the subject of poems.'[10]

I hope I shall not be misinterpreted as dismissing the wealth and variety of good and genuine poetry in England and America in the last thirty or so years because I said it had not produced any works or corpus of works that could be called great art. Literary history shows that it is folly to expect great poets to follow each other in an unbroken sequence. There have been other periods, like the present, in which it would have been difficult for anyone living at the time to foresee the emergence of a new authoritative style, but whose poets we still read with pleasure. In the seventeen-eighties Blake lamented that the Muses had forsaken poetry:

> How have you left the antient love
>   That bards of old enjoy'd in you!
> The languid strings do scarcely move!
>   The sound is forc'd, the notes are few!

In the late eighteen-nineties, Wilde was to declare: 'It is to criticism that the future belongs. The subject-matter at the disposal of creation becomes every day more limited in extent and variety.' Gilbert's stooge, Ernest, in the two dialogues Wilde wrote on 'The Artist as Critic', sums up what Gilbert (that is Wilde) has taught him: 'that criticism is more creative than creation, and that the highest criticism is that which reveals in the work of Art what the artist had not put there.' It sounds like a wonderful anticipation of the most up-to-date criticism; but the specimens provided of Gilbert's creativity as a critic are not very impressive. He gives a rhapsodic summary of the Divine Comedy in the deplorable style of the unfortunate letter to Bosie that Wilde was unable to persuade the insensitive Carson was a 'prose poem'.[11]

The situation seems to be rather the same in the novel, where Joyce and Lawrence have again had no obvious progeny. Neither in America nor in England, although again America has been more adventurous and experimental, has there been anything like the establishment of a group of novelists animated by a common theoretical position, such as the practitioners of the *nouveau roman* in France who derive from the immediate post-war novels of Sartre and Camus. An interesting development in England has been the attraction of the *roman fleuve*, which was very popular in France in the period between the wars. After Proust's masterpiece, there were sequences by Georges Duhamel, Roger Martin Du Gard, and Jules Romains. In England, after the second war, we have had C. P. Snow's sequence, running from 1943 to 1970, which, in spite of Dr Leavis's disapproval, I find curiously impressive, Durrell's *Alexandrian Quartet*, 1957 to 1960, Evelyn Waugh's trilogy, 1952 to 1961, revised by him into a long one-volume novel, *Sword of Honour*, Olivia Manning's *Balkan Trilogy*, 1960 to 1965, Anthony Powell's twelve-volume sequence, *A Dance to the Music of Time*, which ran from 1951 to 1975, and Paul Scott's *Raj Quartet*, 1966 to 1975. With the exception of Durrell's Alexandrian novels and Paul Scott's Indian sequence, these are all in differing degrees a combination of fictionalized auto-biography and contemporary or recent history. Their subject, handled on a large scale, is a man and his times, or man in society. The whole period has also been extremely rich in biography, autobiography, and memoirs, which satisfy needs not catered for by novels written by the alienated for the alienated.

The exception to these generalizations about the modernist movement in England and America, and it is a large one, is the theatre. During the last thirty years the drama has been far more experimental and innovative than poetry and the novel, and it has produced one writer of genius who has completed the modernist enterprise by transferring the symbolic image to the stage. It is, all the same, rather doubtful whether one should regard Samuel Beckett as an English writer (in the sense in which Yeats and Joyce are English writers) or a French writer, since he writes in both languages and lives in Paris. Turning from a series of novels, he has presented on the stage a desolating image of human existence with an intellectual vigour, a genius for the absurd, and a verbal range that takes up the experiment that Eliot abandoned after *Sweeney Agonistes*, which, as has been said, might well have been called *Waiting for Pereira*.[12] Abandoning plot and any localization in place or time, his plays aim radically at a kind of 'pure theatre', offering us simply the experience of a present, the tense of drama, in all its unmitigated meaninglessness: a present in which 'the past is all deception and the future futureless'. Beckett has been called the Master of the Theatre of the Absurd. We have also had, along with the Committed Theatre, the Theatre of Violence, and the Theatre of Cruelty, the Liberated Theatre, in which there is nothing hid that shall not be revealed, and, as some relief, what may be called the Zany Theatre in the intellectual extravaganzas of Tom Stoppard, and television shows such as the original Monty Python's Flying Circus. In these cheerfulness breaks in. And it is needed, for underlying all the variety of this dramatic energy is a dismal philosophy of man trapped by society, or by sexual dilemmas, or by self-destructive urges from which there is no escape except suicide, madness, violence, or a retreat to infantilism or to a mindless liberation through eroticism. It is Beckett's great distinction that he presents, in a strange way, an enterprise that, although impossible to achieve, is yet necessary and heroic—the attempt to make sense.

If biographies, autobiographies, and memoirs have flowed from the presses in the last thirty or so years, so have works of criticism. Yet with the exception of Northrop Frye, whose *Anatomy of Criticism* appeared in 1957, it is difficult to think of any critics who have exercised an influence and authority comparable to that exercised by the most distinguished of the old New Critics. I could run through a long list of writers, mainly, but by no means all, academic, who have most notably fulfilled the function of criticism as Eliot saw it and promoted 'the understanding and enjoyment of literature'; but it is also sadly true that New Criticism has left behind it an enormous army of camp-followers industriously exercising interpretative ingenuity on poems and novels. One of the elder statesmen of the English literary establishment, James Sutherland, wrote in 1974:

I know that the best of twentieth-century literary criticism is better than most of what was available to me as a student; but I also know that a prodigious proliferation of Old Man's Beard has spread over English literature, and that this parasitical growth of structural analysis, explications, views, and new interpretations *begotten by despair upon improbability* too often conceals the work it was presumably intended to reveal.[13]

Some ten years earlier, in what was, alas, her last book, Rosemond Tuve made a similar protest, also using a botanical simile to describe some interpreters of *The Faerie Queene*: 'Some recent explanations of scenes in Spenser require page upon multiplied page of re-phrased argument, unwritten soliloquies added to make complicated motives seem plausible, supposed ejaculations, speeches translated into the tone necessary for the claimed meaning to be there—in short the use of paraphrase to a degree never before attempted in any criticism.' She added in a note: 'It is ironic that this critical method has overgrown the poem, like a sort of carpet of succulents, as an outcome of the appeal to read the "poem as poem".'[14] And if a great deal of these critical interpretations and 'new readings', which proliferate in journals to be gathered together to bemuse the student in *Casebooks*, darken understanding, they also blight enjoyment. The speaker in the following brief poem by Simon Curtis might be taken as expressing the feelings of either a student, who has been enduring, or a lecturer, who has been inflicting on others, a course on the novel:

> The mind's eye aches from Henry James,
> Like arms from heavy cases, lugged for miles.
> *Theme and structure, imagery and tone.*
>
> From Lawrence, too: how hard I dug
> For insights, sunk yards deep, in turgid prose.
> *Theme and structure, imagery and tone.*
>
> Web of necessity in *Daniel Deronda*,
> Gloom in *Dorrit*, gloom in Flaubert,
> One more week to go, at
> *Theme and structure, imagery and tone.*

He is longing for the end of term to come when he can relax

and play over records of that delightful and witty composer, Erik Satie, whose 'good melodic dissonance'

> Will pierce low clouds of syllabus
> With humour's grace,
> Mercy of irreverence.[15]

Having recently read through a draft of a report for the *Shakespeare Survey* of last year's work in Shakespearian criticism, I can more than understand and sympathize with a desire to find a new methodology to succeed the New Critics' attempt to found one. But this new method, which substitutes the microscope for the lemon-squeezer, and replaces the search for 'theme and structure, imagery and tone' by the delight in the infinite play of significances emitted by a text, transforms the defects in the methods of the New Critics into a radical rejection of the concept on which not only literary studies but all sciences, humane as well as natural, depend: that 'there is a possibility of co-operative activity, with the further possibility of arriving at something outside ourselves, which may provisionally be called truth'. I am quoting Eliot again, from the close of his early essay on criticism.[16] He places it firmly here within the great human enterprise of increasing man's knowledge of the world he lives in and of himself. It is the function of the universities to further this by the dissemination and advancement of knowledge. They are, or should be, the intellectual conscience of society. The subjectivism and relativism that accepts any and every reading of a text as equally valid, and declares reading to be the personal importing of meaning into texts, removes criticism from all kinds of intellectual enquiry. There is nothing we can teach, and no distinction between true and false statements, or between understanding and misunderstanding. (This view does, of course, do away with the élitist assumption that some people are better readers than others and some critics more helpful than others in increasing enjoyment and understanding.) The only form of sharing we can hope for is a certain delight and admiration for each other's playfulness and ingenuity. In evacuating literature of determinate meanings, criticism must necessarily deny that its aim is the discovery of truth. It has opted out of the common enterprise, which Sir Peter Medawar describes when he says: 'The scientist values research by the size of its contribution to that huge, logically articulated structure of ideas which is already, though not yet half built, the most glorious accomplishment of mankind. The humanist must value his research by different but equally honourable standards, particularly by the contribution it makes, directly or indirectly, to our understanding of human nature and conduct, and human sensibility.'[17] We must allow Sir Peter to blow the trumpet for scientific research since he has been involved in what is perhaps the greatest advance in knowledge that has come in the last third of this century; and we must thank him for stating so clearly the distinction between science as a structure of ideas of universal application, provisionally true until disproved or modified by new evidence, and the humanist's quest, which is to understand the nature of man as it manifests itself in time and history, in situations which, although they may be compared, never exactly repeat themselves.

It was a main complaint against the old New Critics that they used statements about the nature of poetry which were derived from the theory and practice of modernist poets as if they were of universal application, and could be applied to appraise works by poets who had very different conceptions of what poetry was. But although they much diminished the sense of *idem in alio*, which is one of the pleasures of reading poetry of past ages or poetry in a foreign tongue, and undervalued poetry that is not complex and oblique, they never questioned the value of reading the classics of ages remote from their own. How could they, with Pound and Eliot as their founding fathers? If they were too eager to relate the present to the past, the new methods destroy any distinction. If texts are only black marks on white paper, emitting an endless play of significances, any one text is as good as another for the purpose of picking up these signals, and they all exist in a timeless state awaiting our attention.

It is difficult, at first sight, to see why this French criticism should attract English and American critics, since the literary situation in France is very different from that in England and America. While in all three countries the modernist movement is still alive in music and the fine arts, it is only in France that it has continued to develop strongly in literature and in the cinema. The *nouvelle critique* accompanies the *nouveau roman* and the avant-garde film in which nothing happens and it is left to the viewers to make what they will of what they see. They are not members of an audience, stirred by a common response, but solitary individuals, each alone in his seat, dreamily responding or fantasizing in his private enclosed world. The ardour with which French writers have pursued the full implications of the Romantic entry into the mind of man, as it developed through the nineteenth century into modernism (with its successors Dadaism and Surrealism) to arrive at a total formalism and abstraction, is in keeping with their literary tradition. French literature has always been 'purer' in the aesthetic sense than English, as the French language is 'purer'. Their literary history is marked by a succession of movements animated by clearly thought-out theoretical positions. There is truth in Graham Hough's feeling that the kind of literary campaign that Pound and Eliot waged for a truly 'modern' poetry was something alien to the English literary tradition, which has not been given to movements and manifestos. Again, ever since the seventeenth century the French have jealously guarded their language against intruders. They are still trying to do so, although their attempt to keep out 'Franglais' does not seem very successful. All the same the very word is significant, suggesting how difficult French finds it to domesticate borrowings from other tongues. It was not until 1913 that Robert Bridges founded the Society for Pure English. It was far too late; the damage had been done centuries before. The American colonists took with them a language that was already gloriously impure and which, since the great flood of immigration began, has been happily hospitable to a wealth of foreign words and idioms, which in turn pass back to England. I think myself that the most important and the greatest legacy that poets so different as Yeats, Pound, and Eliot left to their successors was not their theories about the nature of poetry, nor their always only partial adoption of the symbolist aesthetic, but their reinvigoration of the language of poetry by bringing it into relation with contemporary and colloquial speech. Exploiting the full range of the richest vocabulary in the world, they did so on the basis of the rhythms and constructions of the real language of men of their day. Here their influence was wholly salutary and can still be felt.

What then accounts for the appearance of the French new criticism in countries where it seems to have little relevance? Why do we find the old New Critical emphasis on the importance of the reader's response, and the distinction between criticism and scholarship revived in these extravagant terms? It marks, I think, a real loss of belief in the value of literature and of literary study. By some, this is dignified and partly justified by being linked with a universal scepticism about the possibility of any real knowledge of the universe we live in or any true understanding of the world of our daily experience. The indeterminacy of literary texts is part of the indeterminacy of the world, which is, to use Frank Kermode's term, an 'unfollowable world'.[18] I find this conception as impossible to swallow as it is difficult to pronounce. The volume of essays by Medawar which I quoted from was called by him *The Art of the Soluble*. He took the title from a review he had written earlier of a book whose author wondered why scientists seem to shirk really fundamental and challenging problems. To which he had retorted: 'If politics is the art of the possible, research is the art of the soluble.' Those afflicted by the difficulty of arriving at ultimate answers to large general questions about the universe might benefit by taking to heart the advice Sidney Smith gave to melancholics: 'Take short views.' We can make a good deal of sense of the natural world and of the world of human affairs both from what we know and from what we think probable on the basis of our past experience. I am not persuaded of the genuineness of some of the purveyors of this fashionable scepticism. In the search for truth, it is only too easy to throw up our hands in the face of human ignorance, as many of us do in the face of huge human calamities, deciding that as we cannot do very much we cannot do anything. 'Let no smalnesse retard thee;' wrote John Donne, 'if thou beest not a Cedar to help towards a palace, if thou beest not Amber, Bezoar, nor liquid gold, to restore Princes; yet thou art a shrub to shelter a lambe, or to feed a bird; or thou art a plantane, to ease a childs smart; or a grasse to cure a sick dog.'[19] So, also, the fact that there are many great questions beyond our resolution does not prevent us from judging between what is true and what is false, and from modestly enlarging by this process our knowledge of ourselves and the world we live in.

I recognize in others a genuine distress and anguish, a feeling that the long history of Western culture is coming to an end, with a bang perhaps in addition to a whimper, and that the great tradition of English poetry is coming to an end with it. I do not believe this is true, although I can see many reasons why some people do. But I cannot accept that we should project our present malaise onto the past, and disregarding what poets themselves have said and say as merely 'their necessary idealisations', find with Harold Bloom that 'the covert subject of most poetry for the last three centuries has been the anxiety of influence, each poet's fear that no proper work remains for him to perform'.[20]

This makes the poet a member of a purely literary family and world, absorbed in his own self-consciousness as a poet, making poems out of other poems, rather than a man engaged like other men in the business of living, communicating his experience of the world and the values he has found in it through the art whose forms and laws he has learnt from his loving study of the poets of the past. I admire Bloom's passionate love of poetry, his belief in standards of excellence and his courage in applying them, his acceptance of the poet as the true begetter of his poem, and of the poem's objective existence. His work is informed by a high seriousness. Nobody could possibly call his criticism trivial or frivolous. Yet, although I owe to him occasional illuminations of particular poems or lines of poetry, I cannot accept his dismal image of the poet in the last three hundred years wrestling in solitude with his precursors, doomed to increasing disappointment as the centuries go on, any more than I can accept the Deconstructionist image of the reader as importing meanings into texts instead of attending to what he is reading. The first image dehumanizes the poet, the second the reader. If we say, with Harold Bloom, that 'poetry is written by the same natural man or woman who suffers daily all the inescapable anxieties of competition',[21] we are not distinguishing human beings from animals. Competitiveness is not distinctively human. Many animals are competitive and aggressive and fight each other fiercely to defend their little pieces of territory. Leaving on one side the many tributes poets have paid to their great precursors, two who are not usually found in agreement, Blake and Eliot, have declared that between poets and their predecessors 'there is no competition'.[22] The reader, occupied in 'making texts' rather than reading them, has mislaid one of the greatest of human qualities: intellectual curiosity, the desire to enlarge his being by learning about something other than himself.

NOTES

1   *The Classical Tradition in Poetry* (Cambridge, Mass., and London, 1927).
2   *The Rambler*, No. 2.
3   'How could we believe, in fact, that the work is an object exterior to the psyche and history of the man who interprets it?' Roland Barthes, *Critical Essays*, trans. Howard (Evanston, Illinois, 1972), 72.
4   *Critical Inquiry* (Chicago, 1977), III. iii. 195, 6.
5   See Henry Chadwick, *Early Christian Thought and the Classical Tradition* (Oxford, 1966), 7: 'Gnosticism, that sombre and repellent theosophy in which Christian redemption is fused with a pessimistic interpretation of Plato, a dualism drawn from a hellenized version of Zoroastrianism, important elements from heterodox Judaism, the whole being mingled with astrology and with magic as the principle techniques for overcoming the powers of fate.'
  A. D. Nock, while referring to Gnosticism as 'a phenomenon belonging to a particular situation in time and place', writes that 'it may fairly be related to certain human attitudes and predispositions which are extremely widespread. Three such suggest themselves at once: a preoccupation with the problem of evil, a sense of alienation and recoil

from man's environment, and a desire for special and intimate knowledge of the secrets of the universe.' *Essays on Religion and the Ancient World*, ed. Zeph Stewart (Oxford, 1972), ii. 940.

6   *Coleridge* (London, 1953), 93–113.

7   See R. S. Crane, 'Criticism as Inquiry', *The Idea of the Humanities* (Chicago, 1967), ii. 25–44 for an admirable summary of the principles of New Criticism, and a criticism of its methods as 'inappropriate to literature and . . . incompatible with inquiry'.

8   Reprinted in *Selected Essays* (London, 1932), 23–34.

9   Reprinted in *On Poetry and Poets* (London, 1957), 103–18; see particularly pp. 113–15.

10   *The Romantic Image* (London, 1957), 153.

11   *Works*, ed. Foreman (London, 1948), 1054, 1058, and 1035–7, reprinted in *The Critic as Artist*, ed. Richard Ellmann (Vintage Books, New York, 1970), 402, 407, and 375–8.

12   See William B. Spanos, '"Wanna Go Home, Baby?": *Sweeney Agonistes* as Drama of the Absurd', *PMLA*, 85 (January 1970), 8–20.

13   'Viewpoint', *TLS*, 15 March 1974.

14   *Allegorical Imagery* (Princeton, New Jersey, 1966), 414.

15   'Satie at the end of Term', from *On the Apthorpe Road and Other Poems*, by Simon Curtis. I first met the poem in *The New Oxford Book of Light Verse*, ed. Kingsley Amis (Oxford, 1978). Mr Curtis, who is a lecturer in comparative literature at Manchester University, tells me that he takes a 'Special Subject' course on England and France in the 1890s, 'which is by no means a soft option', and 'as a Christmas treat' plays music to the class. 'The poem', he writes, is 'a little teacherly celebration of this Christmas class, sitting in my room, usually on a dour December morning.'

16   *Selected Essays*, 34.

17   *The Art of the Soluble* (London, 1967), 126.

18   *The Genesis of Secrecy* (Cambridge, Mass., 1979), chapter 6.

19   *Essays in Divinity*, ed. Evelyn M. Simpson (Oxford, 1952), 66.

20   *The Anxiety of Influence* (New York, 1973), 148. Bloom's view is a depressing, or to use his own words, 'a splendidly dismal' version of Northrop Frye's dictum: 'Poetry can only be made out of other poems, novels out of other novels.' *The Anatomy of Criticism* (Princeton, New Jersey, 1957), 97.

21   *A Map of Misreading* (New York, 1975), 165.

22   Blake on Wordsworth's 'To H. C. Six Years Old': 'This is all in the highest degree Imaginative & equal to any Poet, but not Superior. I cannot think that Real Poets have any competition. None are greatest in the Kingdom of Heaven; it is so in Poetry.' (*Poetry and Prose*, ed. Geoffrey Keynes, (London, 1927), 1024.) T. S. Eliot, '—but there is no competition—', *East Coker*, 185.

Chapter II

The Relevance of Literature

On the battlefield of Shrewsbury Sir John Falstaff pauses to wonder whatever he is doing there and why he is doing it: 'Well, 'tis no matter; honour pricks me on. Yea, but how if honour prick me off when I come on? How then? Can honour set to a leg? No. Or an arm? No. Or take away the grief of a wound? No. Honour hath no skill in surgery, then? No. What is honour? A word. What is in that word? Honour. What is that honour? Air. . . .' Having thus by his catechism displayed the absolute uselessness of honour for all practical purposes, he declares roundly, 'Therefore I'll none of it.' The speech is witty and justly famous. We laugh at it because we know that it is both true and nonsense. It is true that honour has no skill in surgery, that it cannot build houses, feed the hungry, invent labour-saving devices, or solve the energy crisis; but it is also true that without honour, the respect and esteem of those whose opinion we value, and a sense of our own personal integrity, 'self-esteem grounded in just and right', we sink below the true human level. We become abject and pitiful; at worst, outcasts from society whom nobody trusts. The criterion of practical utility is inappropriate here. We have to judge the value of honour in the sense in which Falstaff uses it by a different standard; not by arguing that without honour commercial dealings between man and man would be impossible—which is true—but by considering the nature of man. The value of honour, like all values, must be argued from our conception of the nature of man, by what it means to be a fully human being.

Few people, I imagine, would provide so crude a yardstick as Falstaff does for measuring the value of literature and the other arts, and would say, as did a friend of mine who was leaving school to begin a medical course while I was staying on to go into the classical sixth, that she could not imagine how anyone could think of giving up a lifetime to the study of literature, which you could read anyhow in your spare time, rather than to something useful like medicine. But a great many people today, including a number of teachers of literature, as well as even greater numbers of students, seem to feel a need to justify literary study by what is only a more subtle form of the utility principle. It lurks behind the current limitation of the word 'relevant' to what has a direct and immediate bearing on what the user considers to be the modern situation. By this some works are elevated as being relevant to current problems, others are relegated to obscurity as being irrelevant to the business of living in the modern world, or, if they are of too great stature to be thus dismissed, are drastically reinterpreted to display their relevance to the concerns of today.

I doubt whether many critics writing today would have the nerve to define poetry as Eliot did in the preface to the second edition of *The Sacred Wood* in 1928 as 'a superior amusement'. 'I do not mean', he explained, 'an amusement for superior people. I call it an amusement, an amusement *pour distraire les honnêtes gens*, not because that is a true definition, but because if you call it anything else you are likely to call it something still more false.'

If we think of the nature of poetry, then poetry is not amusing; but if we think of anything else that poetry may seem to be, we are led into far greater difficulties. Our definition of the use of one kind of poetry may not exhaust its uses, and will probably not apply to some other kind; or if our definition applies to all poetry, it becomes so general as to be meaningless. It will not do to talk of 'emotion recollected in tranquillity', which is only one poet's account of his recollection of his own methods; or to call it a 'criticism of life', than which no phrase can sound more frigid to anyone who has felt the full surprise and elevation of a new experience of poetry. And certainly poetry is not the inculcation of morals, or the direction of politics; and no more is it religion or an equivalent of religion, except by some monstrous abuse of words. . . . On the other hand, poetry as certainly has something to do with morals, and with religion, and even with politics perhaps, though we cannot say what.

It is striking to hear Eliot, a profoundly serious poet both in his dedication to his art and in his exploration through his art of our most serious experiences, moral distress, loneliness, religious doubt, and a faith found 'somewhere on the other side of despair', declaring that the best he could do to define the particular art to which he had dedicated his life—and one must assume he thought the same applied to the other arts—was to call it 'a superior amusement'. As a schoolgirl I found no better answer to my censorious friend, who thought me frivolous to want to give my life to the study of literature: 'But what are the people you cure to do when they get better, or how are the people you can't cure to amuse themselves?'

Amusement, pleasure, enjoyment: these are not popular words today in critical discussion of the arts. They are left to the despised connoisseurs. Nor is Eliot's word 'superior' one that features prominently in our modern vocabulary, although many of those who prudently avoid using it believe in their heart of hearts that some forms of enjoyment, like some kinds of behaviour, are superior to others. But if we understand by enjoyment the satisfaction we find in the exercise of our faculties, physical, mental, and spiritual, enjoyment is far from being a trivial conception. It has been held to be the very end of our being. The old Scottish Shorter Catechism put it that the chief end of man was 'To glorify God and to enjoy him for ever', and the Psalmist declared 'In thy presence is fullness of joy and at thy right hand is pleasure for evermore.' If 'amusement' is now restricted to the more trivial kinds of pleasure, there is one quality amusement shares with the nobler conceptions of pleasure and joy: disinterestedness. We are at least not thinking about ourselves, our wants and our needs, our rights and our wrongs, our health or our grievances, when we are amused. Amusement wonderfully distracts us from our self-concern, takes us out of ourselves, restoring to us, while we are amused, a radical innocence. So I can accept Eliot's definition of poetry as a superior amusement, since it points to what all poetry, whether light verse, minor poetry, or sublime poetry, must at least have, the *unum necessarium*: 'the power of engaging attention and alluring curiosity'. It was the lack of this power that made Johnson declare that the other excellencies of Prior's *Solomon* were 'of small avail'. He went on: 'Tediousness is the most fatal of all faults; negligencies or errors are single and local, but tediousness pervades the whole; other faults are censured and forgotten, but the power of tediousness propagates itself. He that is weary the first hour, is more weary the second; as bodies forced into motion, contrary to their tendency, pass more and more slowly through every successive interval of space.' More succinctly he dismissed Thomson's *Liberty*: '*Liberty*, when it first appeared, I tried to read, and soon desisted. I have never tried again, and therefore will not hazard either praise or censure.' As I grow older, I find myself more and more following Johnson's example. 'If the prospect of delight be wanting (which alone justifies the perusal of poetry) . . .'. This sounds like Johnson again; but it is Eliot wearing his Johnson hat and recommending the reading of Dryden.

The most striking phrase in the passage quoted from Eliot is when he writes of feeling 'the *full surprise and elevation* of a new experience of poetry'. I most value Eliot as a critic, not for his theorizing or for his judgements, but for his delight in poetry and for the catholicity of his taste, which appears as much in his gift for quotation in his essays as in the allusions and echoes in his poetry. This 'full surprise and elevation' that the reader feels 'travels' to him through the words on the page from the author's own delight. I borrow the word 'travel' from Sir Peter Medawar comparing the act of creation in the sciences and the arts.

Certainly 'having an idea'—the formulation of a hypothesis—resembles other forms of inspirational activity in the circumstances that favour it, the suddenness with which it comes about, the wholeness of the conception it embodies, and the fact that the mental events which lead up to it happen below the surface of the mind. But there, to my mind, the resemblance ends. No one questions the inspirational character of musical or poetical invention because the delight and exaltation that go with it somehow communicate themselves to others. Something *travels*: we are carried away. But science is not an art form in this sense; scientific discovery is a private event, and the delight that accompanies it, or the despair at finding it illusory, does not travel. One scientist may get great satisfaction from another's work and admire it deeply; it may give him great intellectual pleasure; but it gives him no sense of participation in the discovery, it does not carry him away, and his appreciation of it does not depend on his being carried away.[1]

When Medawar speaks of the 'delight and exaltation' that go with musical and poetical invention, he is echoing what many poets have told us: from Sidney, who speaks of the poet as 'lifted up with the vigor of his own invention . . . freely ranging onely within the Zodiacke of his own wit', to Wordsworth, declaring that 'in describing any passions whatever, which are voluntarily described, the mind will, upon the whole, be in a state of enjoyment' and Keats, saying of the poetical character that 'it lives in gusto'. Milton's opening prayer was for light as well as for elevation: 'What is dark in me illumine, what is low raise and support', and Dryden, in a splendid passage, too good for the feeble play it prefaces, writes of 'a confus'd Mass of Thoughts, tumbling over one another in the Dark: When the Fancy was yet in its first work, moving the Sleeping Images of Things Towards the Light'. And if we turn to one of the many 'most excellent Poets that never versified', who can read Henry James's Notebooks without feeling the excitement with which, when a *donnée* which had slumbered in his mind pushed itself forward into the light, he set himself to expand it and give it form by his art?

In the first of his studies in the theory of fiction, *The Sense of an Ending*, Frank Kermode called his last chapter 'Solitary Confinement'. He took the title from a remarkable book by Christopher Burney, a British Agent in Occupied France who was caught by the Gestapo. In total solitude in his cell he produced two kinds of fictions. One was a necessity if he were to survive. He invented plausible stories about what he had been up to in France to deceive his interrogators. They had to be completely realistic. To preserve his own sanity he invented fictions of relation, of ends and beginnings, and of concords, to punctuate otherwise meaningless tracts of time—inventing for himself a clock by using the shadow cast by a gable on a wall, which he could see through the fretted glass of a window high up his cell, and telling himself that he would be free by Christmas, and, when Christmas had come and gone and he was still in his cell, fixing on another date. It is a very moving book and the prisoner alone in his cell with the threat of torture and death hanging over him is an all too painfully typical hero of our time. Kermode says that Burney found in his solitude and poverty 'this image of modern art: inconceivable diversity of state without solidarity of plight'. This is possibly a true image of modern art if we apply it to those writers who have carried the modernist movement forward to a complete self-absorption. But when Kermode says that we 'can, if we like think of his [Burney's] book as a model of a more general solitary confinement, of the fictions and interpretations of human beings "doing time", imagining ends and concords',[2] I cannot assent. Can we really think of the desperate condition of Burney, inventing plausible fictions to save his life, and alone in his cell, deprived of all contact with the natural world, and of all commerce with his fellow men, as presenting an image of the human condition, even figuratively? It seems a kind of outrage, an insensibility to real and terrible suffering to relate the extremity in which he found himself to the epistemological anxieties which afflict some modern writers and intellectuals. And is there any true comparison to be made between this notion of man's desperate need to invent fictions to live by in an incomprehensible world and the mastery and creative energy of the great masters of fiction in poetry or the novel, rendering through their art an experience of living which meshes with our own?

A more universal and natural image of the great makers of fictions through the centuries since ''Omer smote 'is bloomin' lyre' is of a mother telling a story to a child: the mother creating, the child responding, the mother delighting in her power of inventing a tale, or in her remaking of an old tale, the child delighting in what has been invented by someone else, and the story as it were floating free between them. The mother tells the tale to please, amuse, or instruct, or to do all three things at once. The child forgets his grazed knee which he was grizzling about, even though it may still ache, or the fact that he had been refused a second sweet or a chocolate biscuit. The mother enjoys her invention and her enjoyment communicates itself to the child. This is a simple and very primitive image of the fundamental pleasure of writing and reading, although it ignores the supposedly impassable gulf between speech and writing, and the author is, of course, present in the flesh to be interrupted and asked questions. It goes, I think, to the heart of the matter. Both mother and child have thrown open the doors of the prison of the present. The mother is wholly concerned with her story, and with telling it in the most lively way; 'devoted, concentrated in purpose' she is making of it a work of art, even if a very humble one. The child is distracted from the clamant needs and desires of childhood; they are temporarily disregarded as his curiosity is aroused. He is learning something in the mos: delightful way, whether the tale is of fairies, or talking animals, or of human beings like those he knows of, or of human beings who lived 'once upon a time'. He is hearing of actions and behaviour that relate to what he already knows, and which he accepts as in some sense true, or let us say as believable: that is, as having some relation to what he knows to be true. The mother has made something which can now have existence in the child's memory. If it has been a story that he has really enjoyed he will ask for it again and again. And as we all know who have had the pleasure of pleasing a child with a tale, there will be trouble if the mother is in a hurry and leaves something out or in any way alters the story.

'The Child is Father of the Man.' I believe with Charles Hoole, a seventeenth-century schoolmaster, 'Tully's observation of old and Erasmus his assertion of latter years that it is as natural for a child to learn as it is for a beast to go, a bird to fly, or a fish to swim.'[3] This is one of the childish things we do not, or should not, 'put away' in growing up. As Auden wrote, rebutting the notion that because it is fair enough to say that A. E. Housman is 'a poet of adolescence' this means that 'nobody over the age of twenty-one can or should enjoy reading him':

To grow up does not mean to outgrow either childhood or adolescence but to make use of them in an adult way. But for the child in us, we should be incapable of intellectual curiosity; but for the adolescent, of serious feeling for other individuals. I can imagine a person who had 'outgrown' both, though I have never met one; he would be a complete social official being without personal identity. All that a mature man can give his child and adolescent in return for what they keep giving him are humility, humour, charity and hope. He will never teach them to despise any strong passion, however strange and limited, or to reject a poet, like Housman, who gives it utterance.[4]

Francis Bacon declared that 'the inquiry of truth, which is the love-making or wooing of it, the knowledge of truth, which is the presence of it, and the belief of truth, which is the enjoying of it, is the sovereign good of human nature'. I would only alter the article and say it is '*a* sovereign good'. For man is not only *animal rationale*, or, to accept Swift's modification of the old definition, *animal capax rationis*, capable of seeking knowledge, of acquiring it, and of enjoying the knowledge of things as they are and not merely as they appear to him; he is also *politikon zōon*, a political animal, that is a social being, a moral being, *capax amoris*. I would like to add to these two ancient definitions that he is also an animal that worships, *capax reverentiae*, capable of feeling reverence and awe, of recognizing excellence, of feeling a sense of freedom from the categories of space and time before what is beautiful, noble, or sublime, and desiring to celebrate, to give thanks, and to praise. Samuel Rogers reports a nicely dry comment here by Grattan, in reply to someone citing Johnson's criticism of *Lycidas* and ending 'Of what use is it?' 'Ah!', said Grattan, 'these things—they take the mind out of the dirt, as it were.'[5] In all three aspects man discovers his full humanity and defines his own identity in his relation to what is other than himself, and in a certain forgetting of himself. C. S. Lewis, in a book of reader-orientated criticism that reflects the experience of a lifelong omnivorous reader, summed up his argument by saying that in reading we 'seek an enlargement of our being. We want to be more than ourselves. . . . We want to see with other eyes, to imagine with other imaginations, to feel with other hearts, as well as with our own,' And he ended by saying:

Literary experience heals the wound, without undermining the privilege, of individuality. There are mass emotions which heal the wound; but they destroy the privilege. In them our separate selves are pooled and we sink back into sub-individuality. But in reading great literature I become a thousand men and yet remain myself. Like the night sky in the Greek poem, I see with a myriad eyes, but it is still I who see. Here, as in worship, in love, in moral action, and in knowing, I transcend myself; and am never more myself than when I do.[6]

The power of literature to liberate the imagination from confinement to present circumstances has never been better shown than by that great imaginative writer Dickens, translating what must have been the experiences of his own unhappy childhood into those of David Copperfield. The sustained cruelty of the Murdstones to the little boy, his alienation through them from his mother made him, he says, 'sullen, dull and dogged'. But for one circumstance he would, he says, 'have been almost stupefied'. The one circumstance was a small collection of books his dead father had left in a little room upstairs which nobody bothered to enter.

From that blessed little room, Roderick Random, Peregrine Pickle, Humphrey Clinker, Tom Jones, the Vicar of Wakefield, Don Quixote, Gil Blas, and Robinson Crusoe came out, a glorious host, to keep me company. They kept alive my fancy, and my hope of something beyond that place and time,—they, and the Arabian Nights, and the Tales of the Genii,—and did me no harm; for whatever harm was in some of them was not there for me; *I* knew nothing of it. . . . It is curious to me how I could ever have consoled myself under my small troubles (which were great troubles to me), by impersonating my favourite characters in them—as I did—and by putting Mr. and Miss Murdstone into all the bad ones—which I did too. . . . I had a greedy relish for a few volumes of Voyages and Travels—I forget what now—that were on those shelves; and for days and days I can remember to have gone about my region of our house, armed with the centre-piece out of an old set of boot-trees—the perfect realisation of Captain Somebody, of the Royal British Navy, in danger of being beset by savages, and resolved to sell his life at a great price. The Captain never lost dignity, from having his ears boxed with the Latin Grammar. I did; but the Captain was a Captain and a hero, in spite of all the grammars of all the languages in the world, dead or alive.[7]

This is the experience of an unhappy child. It finds an echo in the experience of an unhappy man, or, at least, of a man in most unhappy circumstances: Keats, writing to his brother George, far away in America, while he was nursing his younger brother Tom, who was dying of consumption, the disease that had killed their mother and was to kill him.

I feel more and more every day, as my imagination strengthens, that I do not live in this world alone but in a thousand worlds. No sooner am I alone than shapes of epic greatness are stationed around me, and serve my Spirit the office which is equivalent to a King's body guard—then 'tragedy with scepter'd pall, comes sweeping by'. According to my state of mind I am with Achilles shouting in the Trenches, or with Theocritus in the Vales of Sicily. Or I throw my whole being into Troilus, and repeating those lines, 'I wander, like a lost Soul upon the stygian Banks staying for waftage', I melt into the air with a voluptuousness so delicate that I am content to be alone.[8]

That both the fictitious child, David, and the young man, Keats, are turning to literature to escape from harsh realities and present misery cannot be denied. I do not regard this as a sign of weakness, a refusal to face life. On the contrary, I regard it as a sign of the resilience of their spirits, which are able to break out of the prison of the self, and refuse to be bounded by their own present wretchedness. And if we are to sneer at the childish identification of the little David with the resourceful and lively heroes of picaresque fiction, or the gallant British Naval Captains, and his identification of the horrible Murdstones with the defeated villains, as 'wishful thinking', to wish is as natural for human beings as to breathe, and as necessary for our spiritual life as breathing is for our natural life. And David's wishes are good wishes: to wish to be brave, resourceful, and clever, and to make the best of things, and to wish for a world in which enterprise and courage are rewarded by success, and spite, meanness, and cruelty are properly and rightly put down. However much as we grow older we find that things by no means turn out so, it is surely better to hope and to go on hoping than to settle dismally for a world in which things are sure to go wrong for us, so that it is no use to make any effort. It is plain that from his childish

reading David drew courage and hope, and that Keats drew
from his a renewed sense of life as full of possibilities and as
infinitely worth living, however dark the present might be.

I have moved on from Eliot's definition of poetry as 'a
superior amusement' to his owning that, although it is not
'the inculcation of morals' it has 'something to do with
morals'. Since imaginative literature gives us images of
human life and records human experience it is inevitably
full of moral ideas and moral feelings, strongly engages our
moral sympathies, and tests our moral allegiances. But its
effects upon us, as a source and a reinforcement of moral
values, are often most powerful when indirect and in
inverse ratio to the explicitness of an author's moral
purpose. Although there is great pleasure in responding to
the voice of strong moral conviction, it is not the writers
who have a 'palpable design upon us' who most notably
expand our knowledge of the world and of ourselves, but
those who, while they amuse us, evoke our curiosity and
engage our sympathies, involve us in a world of moral
choice and moral values through our 'fond participation' in
imagined adventures, crises, joys and distresses. Nobody
could possibly claim that Roderick Random, Peregrine
Pickle, or Tom Jones were exemplary characters, models of
virtuous conduct. Dickens, well aware that Mr Podsnap
would regard the works in which they appear as very far
from suitable reading for young persons, slips in a sly little
defence—'Whatever harm was in some of them was not
there for me; *I* knew nothing of it'! But nobody, surely,
would deny that, in different ways Smollett and Fielding
share a tone of affirmation,[9] a sense of life as an adventure.
It was to this that the child responded. It is something he
would not have heard if he had been given some improving
work designed to inculcate in him the behaviour expected of
a child of his age and station.

The belief that moral values are only present in works of
literature if the author writes with an explicit moral purpose
is like the stress today on the concept of 'relevance' by
which the importance and value of poems or novels are
assessed by their immediate, and supposedly practical, use
in assisting our understanding of the world today. The

notion that the literature of the twentieth century is particularly relevant in helping us to come to terms with the world of the twentieth century underlies the importance given in many universities to the study of contemporary literature and the demand by students that more and more time should be given to it at the expense of the literature of the past. There is a still more damaging assumption: that we can only find relevance in the works of the past by radical reinterpretations and new readings, by which they can be made to bear directly on our present needs and concerns, so that we can find in them, as modern readers, what we expect to find in modern poems and novels.

Reading is essentially a solitary occupation and our reception of a book is an individual and personal experience. If we are reading in company, in a library, or in a room with others present, we shut them out; and, if we are spoken to, we feel like a diver coming to the surface. We read at our own pace and can vary it according to our pleasure. We can stop to think over what we have just read and reflect or muse over it, or turn back to an earlier passage which what we have just read recalls or seems to modify. There is great pleasure in being part of an audience (at a lecture, or at a concert, or in the theatre): the pleasure of being alone with a book is another thing. Often after having enjoyed a public performance we look forward to reading the lecture, want to play over in solitude a record of what we heard in the concert-hall, or to settle down to read for ourselves alone the play we have just seen. True relevance is always relevance to *me*, something in a poem or a novel that engages me personally so that I can read it again and again at different periods of my life and in quite different circumstances. All devoted and compulsive readers know when this 'click', as I may call it, occurs. They also know that it often does not take place when they would have expected it to, and contrariwise, that it may well do so unexpectedly. It is also true, in my experience, that works that seemed highly relevant when I first read them have lost the quality I found in them and that attracted me now that circumstances have changed. I remember being deeply impressed by Arthur Koestler's *Darkness at Noon* when it first appeared; but the other day I took it up to re-read it and found it unrewarding. My interest had been held by its topicality: it seemed to make humanly comprehensible the fantastic confessions of the old Bolsheviks in the treason trials under Stalin. It still seems to me a clever and serious book, but no more. I wonder what I shall think of *First Circle* and *Cancer Ward* if I ever come to re-read them. I think they may wear better and seem less like solutions to a psychological problem and more like revelations of human behaviour in almost unimaginably inhuman conditions. But I am too near my first reading to say. On the other hand, a book read and enjoyed for its own sake many years ago can in memory, or in re-reading, have a relevance not recognized when it was first read. There are works we grow into and works that grow with us. Real and genuine relevance, like happiness, is most often found when not being looked for.

I am not suggesting anything so absurd as that there is neither profit nor pleasure to be found in reading and discussing contemporary literature. But I do not think it is a very rewarding subject for study in the English departments of universities, or that it provides the most suitable set texts for candidates for public examinations in our schools. I think, also, that there is in many universities a disproportionate emphasis on the study of the admittedly great literature of the first half of this century, as being of peculiar relevance to our understanding of the 'modern mind'. Nearly twenty years ago, in an essay in the *Partisan Review*, Lionel Trilling, in a tone of ironic regret, accepted 'the unargued assumption of most curriculums that the real subject of all study is the modern world; that the justification of all study is its immediate and presumably practical relevance to modernity; that the true purpose of all study is to lead the young person to be at home in, and in control of, the modern world'. This led him to wonder

if perhaps there is not to be found in the past that quiet place at which a young man might stand for a few years, at least a little beyond the competing attitudes and generalizations of the present, at least a little beyond the contemporary problems which he

is told he can master only by means of attitudes and generalizations, that quiet place in which he can be silent, in which he can
know something—in what year the Parthenon was begun, the
order of battle at Trafalgar, how Linear B was deciphered: almost
anything at all that has nothing to do with the talkative and
attitudinizing present, anything at all but variations on the
accepted formulations about *anxiety*, and *urban society*, and
alienation, and *Gemeinschaft* and *Gesellschaft*, all the matter of the
academic disciplines which are founded upon the modern self-
consciousness and the modern self-pity.[10]

This puts admirably the great virtue of studying the
literature of past ages: that it demands that for a while we
lay aside our own concerns, prejudices, and opinions and
enter into the experiences of other by a 'fond participation'.
I have borrowed this phrase from Henry James.[11] I prefer it
to the current phrase by which the test of a book is whether
the reader can, or cannot, 'identify with' the characters of a
novel or the feelings of a poet. This seems to suggest that
we cannot outgrow the egotism appropriate to childhood
and take seriously the reality of the experience of others and
want in some measure, by the power of the imagination, to
share it and feel with it. I am not attempting to be
paradoxical when I give it as my conviction that the study of
the literature of past ages has greater relevance to our ability
to live well and act justly in the modern world than a
concentration on the literature of the present and of the
more immediate past. It enables us to develop individual
values and our own aesthetic criteria; to discover for
ourselves standards of permanence which can save us from
the domination of fashion, and from an uncritical acceptance of the idols of the tribe and of the market place. It
opens our minds to the potentialities of human nature, and
is an exercise in liberality and generosity, if we read with
disinterested attention not to approve or disapprove, not to
argue or refute, or to take up an attitude, but primarily to
'weigh and consider'. We may encounter terrible as well as
splendid possibilities, beliefs we do not share, religious or
political, and societies whose assumptions, manners, and
customs are alien to us. But judgement must wait on
understanding. We impoverish the literature of the past,

and ourselves too, if we are eager to make it accord with our
own convictions, by reinterpreting it in the light of modern
preoccupations, or with our lack of convictions, and lack of
interest in the convictions of others, by treating a work as a
purely aesthetic object which has nothing to say to us:
reading *Emma*, for instance, as a document in the history of
the oppression of women giving us a picture of a lively,
intelligent young woman forced into conformity with a
narrow-minded, male-dominated society, rebuked for expressing her natural impatience with that tedious old Miss
Bates, and dwindling at last into exchanging her role as
good daughter to her silly old fuss-pot of a father for the
estate of being merely 'wife to Mr. Knightley'; or attempting to make it possible for us to enjoy the poetry of George
Herbert by concentrating on his 'strategies', as if a poet
were a kind of magician or illusionist, and a critic's main
task were to explain how 'it is all done by mirrors'.

A slightly different, but equally disabling, approach is the
exaggeration of the truth that we are persons of the
twentieth century who cannot divest ourselves of the immense changes in knowledge, thought, and sensibility that
separate us from men of past ages to 'follow an antique
drum', into the idea that we must inevitably read the
literature of the past with the demands and expectations we
bring to the literature of our own age. In his Eliot lectures
at Canterbury, given in 1973 and published in 1975 under
the title *The Classic*, Frank Kermode took up the theoretical
position that for us a classic is any work that is still read
after a hundred years, and that is susceptible of infinite
interpretations, can be remade to speak to us today, and
remade again and again to speak to generations to come. He
takes as seriously intended the test of a century, which
Horace cited only to mock at it, and arrives at the notion
that the status of a classic is not given through the centuries
by the judgement of the common reader, but by the
possibility of its providing sufficient material for a
Casebook. Neither Johnson, proposing as the only test of
value 'continuance of esteem', and rejoicing 'to concur with
the common reader' in praise of Gray's Elegy, nor Virginia
Woolf, taking Johnson's phrase for the title of her essays in

criticism, was appealing to a popular as opposed to an élitist judgement. They were appealing, against judgements by academies or professional critics, to the free judgement of those who read widely for enjoyment and find confirmation and extension of their own experience and values in what they read as a main element in their enjoyment. Both assume they are writing for persons who have read widely. Johnson is more concerned with what he feels to be generally and always true out of his own experience of life; Virginia Woolf is more concerned and delighted by human oddity and particularity; but in both there is the same appeal 'from criticism to nature'.

Turning from a discussion of Virgil through the ages, since Eliot had taken Virgil as the great European classic, Kermode, in his third lecture, considered Hawthorne as, by his standard, a modern classic. Some years earlier, in 1964, Lionel Trilling wrote an essay on 'Hawthorne in Our Time',[12] in which he pondered on Henry James's monograph on Hawthorne, written for the English Men of Letters Series, and published in 1879, and compared James's Hawthorne with the Hawthorne presented in *A Casebook on the Hawthorne Question*, edited by Agnes Donohue in 1962. He quotes the editor's preface, which declares that the stories and sketches gathered together in the *Casebook* 'disclose a signal ambiguity in Hawthorne—his attitude towards man's moral nature'. She sees Hawthorne's 'ambivalence about guilt and innocence' as a 'lodestone that draws into its magnetic field other problems of human life'. He writes of 'man's dark odyssey in an alien world'. And she concludes: 'Many of the tales or romances, as he thought of them, are multi-leveled, ironic explorations of the human psyche—capable of endless extensions of meaning and of stimulating repeated analysis and interpretation.' Trilling, comparing the two views of Hawthorne—Henry James's 'ironical entertainer . . . a graceful and charming figure as he amuses himself with the toys strewn over the playground of a disused morality', and Professor Donohue's 'grave, complex, and difficult Hawthorne'—at first admits that 'we must, in all humility, feel that ours is the right one, or, at least for us, the inevitable one'. For, he asks, 'how can any member of the literary community fail to conclude that there is an intrinsic superiority' in the Hawthorne who tells us of 'man's dark odyssey in an alien world' to the Hawthorne who thought of himself as writing tales or romances and the Hawthorne of Henry James? Trilling means, of course, by 'the literary community', the academic community, today's literary establishment. It does not include those odd persons who take down a volume of Hawthorne from the shelves of a public library and read him without guidance.

But Trilling was a cunning and ambivalent critic, and at the close, after some hedging, he rounds on himself. If we try to read Hawthorne as we read Kafka, Hawthorne 'is manifestly inferior to Kafka'. His imagination is not 'boldly autonomous'; it does not confront 'subjective fact only'. 'Over Hawthorne's imagination the literal actuality of the world always maintains its dominion.' For Hawthorne 'always consented to the power of his imagination being controlled by the power of the world'. In the middle of his essay Trilling had confessed that 'in having busied ourselves to discover' that Hawthorne 'is a Question, which then we must bestir ourselves to answer, we have lost much of the charm and fragrance which may well be his essence'. And he added: 'One cannot have everything, but whoever has first read Hawthorne in childhood—James makes a point of his having done so—will be inclined to feel that something he once knew is missing, something that spoke to him, and very movingly, before ever ambiguity was a word, some wind or music of unparticular significance that had its abode in the forests and haunted the Notch and played around the Great Stone Face.' Summing up, Trilling concludes that 'if we tell the truth about our experience of Hawthorne, some of us will say that as we read him—or at moments as we read him—we have a sensation of having been set at liberty'. Owning that this is not an 'entirely comfortable condition' and we 'find ourselves at a loss and uncertain when we are in the charge of an artist so little concerned to impose upon us the structure of his imagination', he adds: 'Yet perhaps we feel, too, an impulse of exhilaration charging through our art-saturated minds, a new pleasure in being led carelessly or playfully to one or another dangerous place and being left alone to look at the danger in our own way.' And he ends by saying that perhaps Hawthorne is 'not for us today, and perhaps not even to-morrow. He is, in Nietzsche's phrase, one of the spirits of yesterday—and the day after to-morrow.' It sounds a sad conclusion: that we either find ourselves forced to make over the literature of the past and, in doing so, are disappointed to find it inferior to the literature of our own day, or we had better lay it aside, since it is only a few, 'some of us', who find in it 'the sensation of being set at liberty'. In the three years that had passed since Trilling wrote the essay I quoted from earlier, the skies had darkened, and it may sound as if he had lost faith in the past as 'that quiet place where a young man might stand'. But I think this would be a misreading of what I see as a gentle protest against an inability to meet an author on his own terms and delight in what he has to give. For, in addition to his recognition of what we lose when we insist on reading Hawthorne in 'our modern way', Trilling provides a beautiful analysis of what Hawthorne can offer to a reader who will read him on his and Henry James's assumption: 'that the world is *there*: the unquestionable, inescapable world; the world so beautifully and so disastrously solid, physical, material, "natural"'.

As well as giving us the sense of liberation from present anxieties and personal concerns, and enabling us to discover standards and values by which current shibboleths can be tested, knowledge and understanding of the past as it survives in works of art, and pre-eminently in literature, enriches our sense of our own identity. Most of us who have lived beyond the meridian of life have experienced what a disaster losing his memory can be for a human being: that he has in large measure ceased to be, and feel himself to be, a person. We know that the persons we now are have become as we are by reason of our personal past. But, as well as this personal past, going back to early childhood, we have also learnt about our family past, the experiences of our parents and grandparents to go no further back. Most children are fascinated by the tales their grandparents tell them of the life they lived, the things they saw and did when they were children. It is something quite different from learning history at school from history-books or from classes in social history, because it comes as lived experience—what it felt like to have been brought up on a farm, or in the slums of a great city, or in a large house with a staff of servants, or in an orphanage sixty or more years ago. Henry James called this past, the past of two generations back, 'the visitable past'. It is the setting of many great novels: *Waverley, or 'Tis Sixty Years Since, Vanity Fair, Middlemarch,* and *War and Peace.* These are not thought of as historical novels because they are built on what was still in living memory for their authors. As we grow older we become aware of an older past that is beyond the memory of the living, and realize that we are the heirs of this too. Literature of all the arts has the power to take us back into what is felt like to live in past ages, and to discover certain constancies in human experience surviving through changes in ideals, beliefs, manners, customs, and social and economic systems.

Beyond our gain as individuals, the dissemination of knowledge and understanding of the past through its literature is a prime source of a society's sense of its own identity and cohesion, something very precious without which it can become a mere ant-heap or beehive devoted to the increase of the Gross National Product. The sense of national identity is not to be confused with a crude nationalism, or desire for national aggrandizement, or contempt for other nations. It is a sense of certain values, characteristic attitudes, on which our sense of community and of belonging depends. This becomes apparent in times of national danger. Thus Wordsworth, in the crisis of the Napoleonic wars, while well aware of his country's failures and errors, saw in her resistance to the despotism of Napoleon the expression of what was finest in the tradition of those who spoke the tongue of Shakespeare and shared with Milton a passion for liberty. Well over a century later, many people in England turned to Wordsworth's 'Sonnets on Liberty and Independence' at an even more critical time, in a struggle against a worse despotism than Napoleon's.

Wordsworth also, in a haunting passage in *The Prelude*, gives with great vividness the sense of desolation, of desertion felt in one's inmost being, when the bond that binds one to one's neighbourhood and country is broken. When Britain 'put forth all her free-born strength in league' with the defenders of the old order to destroy the young French Republic, on which Wordsworth had set all his hopes for the future of the human race, he found himself rejoicing

> When Englishmen by thousands were o'erthrown
> Left without glory on the field, or driven
> Brave hearts! to shameful flight. It was a grief—
> Grief call it not, 'twas anything but that,—
> A conflict of sensations without name. . . .

And in the village church, when prayers were offered for his country's soldiers or praises for their victories, he

> like an uninvited guest
> Whom no one owned, sate silent, shall I add
> Fed on the day of vengeance yet to come.

Times of acute danger, or times of such deep conflicts of conscience as Wordsworth endured, are fortunately not always with us. In happier times there works almost unconsciously and subtly a sense of certain long-established virtues, ways of behaviour, and modes of feeling that are ours by long inheritance. Like all good things this can become perverted and take vulgar and evil forms. Expressions such as 'un-British' or 'un-American' can express hateful attitudes of bigotry and intolerance; but those who use such terms are not usually persons who have opened their minds by any very wide or deep reading in their countries' literature, which might have given them a fuller sense of the virtues inherent in 'the British way of life' or 'the American experience'. The need of a society to have knowledge of its past through its literature is seen very clearly in the desire of the developing countries in Africa to preserve, by writing it down, the oral literature in which their own past lives.[13] Nobody could think that this had any relevance to the grave political and economic problems facing the emergent African states; but it is plainly felt by them to have great relevance to their sense of identity, their dignity and status as human societies. V. S. Naipaul, in a series of essays collected together under the title of *The Return of Eva Peron*, has presented a sombre picture of what happens to societies that substitute grandiose fantasies about their past for a true knowledge of their own history.

The present tendency to stress the literature of the twentieth century at the expense of the literature of earlier times, and the attempt to remake the literature of the past in the image of the present, is to give young people a mess of pottage for their birthright. Their years at school and at the university are the years when they should be filling up their camel's hump, taking in nourishment that will sustain them through years when practical necessities and the duties of their daily lives may leave them little time for concentrated reading. All good teachers want to have students who read widely for themselves, and are happy to talk with them about their reading and to learn from them; but it is the responsibility of teachers to choose what works are to be studied, as being of primary importance and of value both in themselves and in their influence on succeeding generations. The heart of any good curriculum in literature must be what has proved through the ages its wearability, and its power to liberate, illuminate, and support. The young can be trusted to find its true relevance for themselves.

Looking back over my own life, and reflecting on 'the enlargement of our being' that C. S. Lewis said we seek in our reading, I think first of the enlargement of the capacity to express ourselves. This goes back for me to a time before I could read for myself. I can remember the enchantment I found in the word 'soporific' when *The Flopsy Bunnies* was read to me. It was applied, I believe correctly, by Beatrix Potter to lettuce. It is a pity that many books for small children today are written in a thin and flat style, and do not stimulate curiosity about words and a desire to adventure with them. As fundamental is the feeling of personal elevation—the heightening of our natural capacities—that great writers can give. I think of the pure feeling of exhilaration that the overflowing exuberance of Dickens's power of invention gives me. It constantly goes far beyond the possibilities of expectation, enlarging the capacity of the reader to marvel at the absurdities, and delight in the idiosyncrasies, of human beings. This response also goes back to my childhood. I remember how, after the air-raids of the first World War, my father would return from patrolling the streets and would read an episode from *The Pickwick Papers*, as a treat, while my brothers and I were drinking our hot milk before going upstairs to bed. The exhilaration I found when a little later I read Dickens for myself is still there whenever I re-read him. I find myself laughing aloud, invaded by a sudden sense of glory; whether I find myself following the remniscent ramblings of Mrs Nickleby, or the quite different, unpunctuated streams of inconsequence that pour from Flora Finching, or am startled by the concentrated, senile malice of Mr F.'s Aunt's rare interjections. Even more wonderful is Mr Pecksniff's capacity to improve any and every occasion—to 'be moral', 'to contemplate existence'. This arouses a feeling that is almost awe. Even when intoxicated he is still driven by 'an irrepressible desire for the improvement of his fellow creatures that nothing could subdue', and, feeling a cooling and refreshing draught playing around his bare legs, is instantly moved to reflect upon legs: 'The legs of the human subject, my friends, are a beautiful production. Compare them with wooden legs and observe the difference between the anatomy of nature and the anatomy of art.' An even greater sense of wonder is aroused by the surrealist flights of Mrs Gamp—such a bravura passage as she launches into when she shakes her umbrella at the 'Ankworks package', wishing it was in 'Jonadge's belly', making a pioneering protest against the growth of technology and the injustices of a male-dominated society:

Them confusion steamers has done more to throw us out of our reg'lar work and bring ewents on at times when nobody counted on 'em (especially them screeching railroad ones), than all the other frights that ever was took. I have heerd a one young man, a guard upon a railway, only three years opened—well does Mrs. Harris know him, which indeed he is her relation by her sister's marriage with a master-sawyer—as is godfather at this present time to six-and-twenty blessed little strangers, equally unexpected

and all of 'um named after the Ingeins that was the cause. Ugh!
one might easy know you was a man's inwention, from your
disregardlessness of the weakness of our natur, so one might you
brute!

There is, of course, far more in Dickens than this; for
instance, his power to invest human beings and the land-
scapes in which we meet them with the quality of the
sinister, which is the reverse side of his delight in human
absurdity. But this is something no other novelist gives us
in such profusion: what Chesterton, commenting on the
'*bounce* of Trabb's boy', described as 'the unconquerable
rush and energy in a character'. Henry James I came to
much later in life, in my thirties, to discover in myself as I
read him a capacity for subtlety and indirection in responding to, and reflecting on, human relations, a power of
suspending or postponing approval or disapproval, a refine-
ment of my moral sensibility, which James appeals to but
does not constrain. About the same time I first read
Trollope, a great novelist of the affections and of the duties
of daily life, showing us men and women involved in a
whole network of relations, personal, local, and professional. He does not, like Dickens, astonish and extend the
imagination of his readers, nor does he, like James, make
great demands upon their attention, stimulating them to a
finer awareness of the beauty of the natural world and the
beauty that is in the achievements of civilization, as well as
to a finer discrimination in the world of moral choices and
decisions. James applied the adjective 'trustworthy' to
Trollope. Although he meant it as faint praise, it is, I think,
true that in reading Trollope we trust both the tale and the
teller, and that this is a great part of the pleasure he gives.
We enjoy the solidity of the persons he creates, the
verisimilitude of the world they move in, and the reality of
the dilemmas they face. We also enjoy the good terms he is
on with his characters and his readers, his shrewd, often
ironic, but never cynical, comments on them and on the
human nature we share with them. What I gain from his
novels, in addition to continuous entertainment, is something I can only call wisdom.

These are three of the novelists I find myself most often

re-reading, if I confine myself to novelists writing in English. Yet for all the pleasure and rewards I find in reading novels, it is in the experience of reading poetry that I find the deepest pleasure and the greatest rewards. In poetry language reaches its highest expressiveness. Meaning is carried into the heart and the mind by the pulse of its rhythms, by repetition and echo, by the sweetness or force of rhyme and assonance, and by the sense we have of difficulty surmounted with ease and of limitation made a source of fullness. These things combine to give it another precious quality, memorability, so that we come to possess it, and, with it, capabilities beyond our natural powers. Something of Milton's mastery of language communicates itself to me as I move with him through a long, winding, periodic sentence, which continually defeats the expectation of a close, until at last with a sense of triumph I arrive at the true close. I too have soared, with no middle flight, and guided down have come safely to rest.

C. S. Lewis said that we read because 'we want to see with other eyes, to imagine with other imaginations. to feel with other hearts'. In the very greatest writers I am less conscious that I am seeing the world through their eyes than of the reality, solidity, and fullness of the worlds they create, and of their truth to my experience of myself and of my neighbours. Of them we can say, as Dryden said of Chaucer, 'Here is God's plenty.' He said also of him that he 'must have been a man of the most wonderfully comprehensive nature', using the same adjective he had applied over thirty years before to Shakespeare, 'the man of all modern, and perhaps ancient people, who had the largest and most comprehensive soul'. Johnson, in his fine expansion of Dryden's tribute, said of Shakespeare's plays that they exhibited 'the real state of sublunary nature' and expressed 'the course of the world'. In declaring as 'the praise of Shakespeare, that his drama is the mirrour of life', he went on in words that are very apposite today: 'he who has mazed his imagination, in following the phantoms which other writers raise up before him, may here be cured of his delirious extasies, by reading human sentiments in human language, by scenes from which a hermit may estimate the transactions of the world, and a confessor predict the progress of the passions.' 'It is impossible', wrote Charles Lamb, 'for the mind to conceive of a mad Shakespeare.'[14] Lamb had every reason, as Johnson had, to regard madness with dread, and to think of 'the uncertain continuance of human reason' as the 'most dreadful and alarming' of the uncertainties of our present state, and not as a privileged source of illumination. Some years ago it could have been said that it was equally impossible for the mind to conceive of an 'alienated Shakespeare'; but today it seems that many minds find it only too easy. Drummond reported Ben Jonson as saying that 'Shakespeare wanted art'. Like Chaucer and other supremely creative artists, Shakespeare is not self-conscious, does not demand that we recognize and admire his virtuosity. The same complaint of 'wanting art' is brought against others of his kind: novelists such as Scott and Dickens and Balzac, who, like Shakespeare, are universal writers of great scope and worldwide influence, creators of worlds which they make us free of.

We cannot claim the status the whole world has agreed to give to Shakespeare for Chaucer, Spenser, or Milton. But in both *Paradise Lost* and *The Faerie Queene* I have the same sense of being given 'God's plenty', a generous excess, 'good measure, pressed down, shaken together, running over', as I have in reading *The Canterbury Tales*. Although the ways through which we are guided in the 'delightfull land of Faery' are the ways of a Never-never Land, Spenser continually engages our experience of living in the quotidian world. Lamb, in the same essay, said 'the things and persons of the Fairy Queen prate not of their "whereabout". But in their inner nature, and the law of their speech and actions, we are at home and upon acquainted ground.' Spenser domesticates the magical, the romantic, and the mythical within our human experiences: of fear and delight, of loving and being loved, of effort and rest after toil, of despair and of the renewal of hope, of living by faith, and of a longing for perfection, for a 'light in which there is no darkness at all'. Johnson was willing to grant that in *Paradise Lost* 'we read a book of universal knowledge'.

More warmly, William Empson, with whom I am delighted
to find myself in agreement, wrote that Milton, in *Paradise
Lost*, 'keeps alive all the breadth and generosity, the welcome to every noble pleasure, which had been prominent in
European history just before his time'. I would only expand
this to say that all the great values of European civilization,
from its roots in ancient Greece, are alive in *Paradise Lost*,
the last fruit of the revival of learning at the Renaissance:
most of all, belief in reason and in man's freedom to choose
or refuse. And, in defiance of Johnson, who complained that
Paradise Lost 'comprises neither human actions nor human
manners', and that, consequently, 'the want of human
interest is always felt', I find a weight of knowledge of men
and of human affairs, and a weight of suffering as well as a
response to human achievement, in Milton's poem, along
with his sense of the beauty and wonder of the created
universe. Chaucer, Spenser, Shakespeare, and Milton are
our supreme masters of wisdom and eloquence, renewing in
us every time we turn to them our sense of the value to be
found in living, and of the beauty that is mediated to us by
our senses. And, by giving us 'new acquist / Of true
experience', they school the heart and the conscience. They
are the common inheritance of all to whom English in any
of its modern forms is a native language, and the great
sources of the poetic powers of later poets.

I am not attempting to claim that literature provides a
way of salvation, or that those who study literature will by
their study attain moral superiority over those who study
other subjects, or will emerge better balanced, less 'susceptible to nervous shock'. Common observation cannot be
called on to support any such view. But neither can I regard
literature as morally neutral. Going up to London to give
evidence for the defence in the trial of Penguin Books for
publishing *Lady Chatterley's Lover*, I met a friend on the
train and told him I was bound for the Old Bailey. He said,
'I do hope you are not going to say that books can do no
harm; for if so, you must believe that they cannot do any
good.' What good it is that they do I find as hard to define
as Eliot did; but I remember that, lecturing here, he found
himself compelled to give the palm among poets of the later

eighteenth century to Johnson, above Gray and Collins, for 'a moral elevation only just short of the sublime'. 'Who prop, thou ask'st, in these bad days, my mind?', Arnold enquired. It is surely a strong contender for the worst opening line of a sonnet in English; but the modest verb 'prop' seems to me well chosen. It was at a time perhaps more bleak than the present that Auden celebrated the poet's supportive role, writing on the death of Yeats, the greatest poet in the English tongue of this century. He died in January 1939, in the dreadful interim between the shame and disgrace of Munich and the outbreak of the war in Europe: 'He disappeared in the dead of winter. . . . The day of his death was a dark cold day.'

> In the nightmare of the dark
> All the dogs of Europe bark,
> And the living nations wait,
> Each sequestered in its hate;
>
> Intellectual disgrace
> Stares from every human face,
> And the seas of pity lie
> Locked and frozen in each eye.
>
> Follow, poet, follow right
> To the bottom of the night,
> With your unconstraining voice
> Still persuade us to rejoice:
>
> With the farming of a verse
> Make a vineyard of the curse,
> Sing of human unsuccess
> In a rapture of distress:
>
> In the deserts of the heart
> Let the healing fountains start,
> In the prison of his days
> Teach the free man how to praise.

NOTES

1　*The Art of the Soluble*, 154–5.
2　*The Sense of an Ending* (New York, 1967), 173 and 164.
3　*A New Discovery of the old Art of Teaching School* (1660).

4 *New Statesman*, 18 May 1957, quoted by Christopher Ricks in the preface to *A. E. Housman* (Englewood Cliffs, New Jersey, 1968).

5 *The Table Talk of Samuel Rogers*, ed. G. H. Powell (London, 1903), 137–8.

6 *An Experiment in Criticism* (Cambridge, 1961), 137 and 140–1.

7 *David Copperfield*, chapter 4.

8 *Letters*, ed. M. Buxton Forman (Oxford, 1941), 241.

9 This is how Auden saw the poet's role:

> Defenceless under the night
> Our world in stupor lies;
> Yet, dotted everywhere,
> Ironic points of light
> Flash out wherever the Just
> Exchange their messages:
> May I, composed like them
> Of Eros and of dust
> Beleaguered by the same
> Negation and despair,
> Show an affirming flame.
>
> 'September 1, 1939'

10 'On the Teaching of Modern Literature', *Beyond Culture* (New York, 1965, London, 1966), 4, 5–6.

11 See the preface to *The Princess Casamassima*.

12 It was written for *Hawthorne Centenary Essays* (Columbus, Ohio, 1964) and reprinted in *Beyond Culture*, pp. 179–208.

13 See the titles in the Oxford Library of African Literature, published by the Oxford University Press. When, during my time as a Delegate of the Press, the question was raised of whether a series that was financially so unprofitable could be continued in difficult times, the answer was that it was published at the express desire of our African branches and was a service we owed to them.

14 'Sanity of True Genius', *The Last Essays of Elia*.

Chapter III

Shakespeare in the Directors' Theatre

If by some powerful magician I were offered transportation to Stratford-upon-Avon around 1612 or so, and promised that I might see Shakespeare on the condition that I should ask him only one question, I know what that question would be. I should not enquire into his relations with his wife, nor ask him to tell me the identity of the Fair Young Man or the Dark Lady, nor should I ask him whether he was at heart a Papist, a Protestant, or a Sceptic. I should not ask him for his brief views on anything at all—either the importance of order and degree in society, or the position of women, or the proper relation of parents and children, or whether he thought power always corrupts—nor should I ask him to outline for me his conception of 'the tragic view of life' or, for that matter, 'the comic'. I should want to ask him why he had appeared to take so little interest in the publication of his plays, and had apparently gone to no trouble to oversee the printing of those that had appeared; and had he any intention, now that he had left London and retired to the country, to produce a volume of his works to include those still unpublished, as well as corrected versions of those that had appeared? Or was he quite indifferent to the idea of fame after death, of leaving behind him something the world would not willingly let die, and had he no care whether, if his works were to survive, they would survive in maimed form—the verse mismetred, many lines unintelligible, speeches wrongly assigned, intended cuts ignored, and cuts made purely for dramatic convenience retained? This is to me the great Shakespearean mystery. It is not because I have spent much time dealing with another writer who also neglected to publish those of his works we now most value, and am therefore professionally concerned with textual problems; nor is it because I am disturbed by the idea that it may be true that our greatest poet 'for gain not glory winged his roving flight', or, as Logan Pearsall Smith put it, at the idea of 'this demi-God, serenely running a popular show and raking in the pennies'.[1] I do not see any necessary connection between poetic genius and financial incompetence. I do not imagine either that, having spent his life writing for a popular as well as for a courtly audience, Shakespeare would have shared, as Donne did, the aristocratic feeling that it was beneath the dignity of a gentleman to condescend to print. I think that there are two possible answers I might get. One would suggest that Shakespeare thought of the plays he had written as essentially scripts for performances, to live on, if they lived at all, through the interpretations of actors, and that he simply did not envisage that a time would ever come in which people would read plays as they read and pored over poems, and histories, and sermons. He did, after all, publish his two narrative poems in good texts. Or, perhaps, the answer I got would suggest that Shakespeare was truly indifferent to the idea of future fame; that he had written out of the fullness of his mind, and a love of writing, of inventing, shaping, and making, and that having made something he felt no further interest in what he had made, because his mind was absorbed in what he was going to do next; and that now he felt the time had come to live at ease, out of the hurly-burly of London, the bustle of the theatre, the pressure to produce plays for his company, and that he was content to leave it to his fellows to do what they wished with the plays he had written for them, and of which they were legally the owners. I think that this last is the most probable explanation: that Shakespeare had the reward he wanted in the exercise of his genius and the success of his plays on the stage and was content with that. The very idea of Shakespeare, like Jonson, editing his own works is inconceivable. The immense force of invention, of imaginative energy, and of linguistic creativeness that gave us this great corpus of plays of such extraordinary variety in not much more than twenty years seems quite incompatible with the patience needed for revision and correction, the tidying up of loose ends, the removal of inconsistencies, the rewriting of what was obscure or carelessly phrased.

Whatever the reason, what we have are essentially scripts for performance, varying greatly in length, and in what we can deduce about the copy from which they were set. However highly we may regard the text of some of the quartos, and however we acknowledge gratefully the care and pains of Heminge and Condell, we cannot regard the plays of Shakespeare, as they are presented to us in modern editions based on the labours of editors during the last two and a half centuries, in quite the same way as we regard the works of an author who prepared his work for the press and oversaw its production to ensure that he was read as he wished to be read. When we read a Shakespearean play, we have to bear in mind as a primary fact that what we are reading was written to please, amuse, thrill, and move, to laughter or to tears, a living audience. And, moreover, the characters were created in order to be recreated by actors, addressing themselves to a motley collection of persons which, by their art, they have to make into an audience that will be delighted, shocked, or moved, in common, however varied the responses of individual members of the audience may be. For in the theatre, the enjoyment of the most intelligent, subtle, and aware, who have studied the play for years and have seen it acted again and again, is dependent, in some degree, on the sympathetic response of others, some of whom may not know the play at all. A fidgety, restless audience, which laughs in the wrong places, or whose apathetic boredom communicates itself, affects the actors, and makes difficult a proper concentration; whereas the hush of an audience that is truly absorbed in the play gives an experience that is comparable to the experience of public worship, in which individuals are united while remaining themselves. The actors, by their imaginations and their art, have to create the illusion of persons whose actions, although they may be unexpected, are yet 'in character', and whose words, although often very far beyond, and sometimes contrary to, expectation—who would expect Beatrice to say 'Kill Claudio!'?—are yet also 'in character'. 'Language', wrote Ben Jonson, 'most shewes a man: speake that I may see thee. . . . No glasse renders a mans forme, or likenesse, so true as his speech.'[2]

Reading, as I have said, is essentially a solitary and private experience, and this is as true of reading a play as it is of reading a novel. Even so, there is a great difference between the way we know a character as we read a play and the way we know a character as we read a novel. The novelist can describe the physical appearance of a character, describe his gestures, tell us in what tone of voice he spoke, and with what emotions, and for what purpose. Most of all he can enter the mind of his characters, both by recounting directly what thoughts passed through their minds, and by using what is now called *le style indirect libre* by which the author moves in and out of the mind of a character without translating its movements into an ordered sequence. The novelist can and often does guide us towards analysis of a character, of a temperament, or personality, or at least provide us with material for such an analysis. In a play by Shakespeare the *dramatis personae* are simply labelled, rather than described: by their office—Theseus, Duke of Athens; or by their relation to another character—Egeus, father to Hermia; or by their generic type—Iago, a villain— Lucio, a fantastic. Sometimes we pick up descriptive phrases from other characters, and comments whose reliability we have to assess, but they are often very general, as are the final tributes in the tragedies. We have come to terms with what is shown to us in act and above all in speech. The soliloquies in Shakespeare's plays are not streams of consciousness, thoughts inconsequently tumbling over one another in the dark. They are sequential, rationally ordered, in language that 'shows' the man. They are addressed as it were to the world, that is, in the performance, to the listening audience. Some are explanatory or proleptic, giving us necessary information or pointing forward to guide us through what we are to see. Some, like those of Richard III and Iago, invite us to share, with a kind of complicity, in the ingenuity and witty resourcefulness of the main agent of the action, the creator of the plot. The great soliloquies of Brutus, Hamlet, Othello, and Macbeth are a main means of ensuring that fond participation by which we are drawn into the very heart of the action through the mind that is most 'finely aware and richly responsible' of all those who act and suffer in the play, and who by feeling most, and masterfully articulating those feelings, articulates ours. Even when Shakespeare enters 'the awful privacy of the insane mind' his characters still address themselves to a world: sometimes, as Ophelia does, to a world that is partly the world around them and partly the world of memory or of fantasy, sometimes to a world wholly conjured up by the imagination, as when Lear holds his assize. Lady Macbeth mutters to herself in an awful solitude, unaware of the presence of the doctor and of her waiting woman, flitting between the present and the past. But she does not reflect upon the past; she lives again the night of the murder and of the banquet, speaking to her husband as if he were by her side. When Eliot stigmatized the 'self-consciousness and self-dramatization of the Shakespearean hero, of whom Hamlet is one',[3] he was treating as a moral defect in the hero, or a moral obliquity in his creator, an essential quality of a fully conceived dramatic character, who communicates to us his consciousness of himself as an actor on the great stage of this world, seeing himself so that we may see him, and expressing himself in language that 'shows' him. This language that 'shewes a man', springs, Jonson said, 'out of the most retired and inward parts of us, and is the Image of the Parent of it, the mind'. By 'the mind' Jonson did not mean the unconscious. He meant the conscious mind, interpreting the reports of the senses, ordering the stores of memory, and employing the powers of fantasy. The great reward of the reader, alone with the text, is that he can make the language yield up all its riches, that he can pause and reflect, resist the onward thrust of the play by turning back or by leaping forward to find echoes and connections, between scene and scene, or speech and speech; he can concentrate his attention on tracing how a single character reveals his or her self in act and in language throughout the play. But, in the end, the reader must go back and accept the current of the play, and allow himself to be borne along with it, responding to all that it gathers into its movement towards the close, not as clues in a problem that by the end of the play will have been solved, but as contributing to an experience to be imaginatively lived through to its full close when all will have been shown. He will find, if he thus yields himself up to the course of the play—goes with its current as it flows, now fast, now slow, now in an eddy, now seeming to break its banks before returning to its main course, with his understanding enriched by all his reading has given him—certain fundamental simplicities remaining from his first experience of the play, whether in reading or in the theatre. These fundamental simplicities are what have kept Shakespeare's plays alive on the stage through the centuries and by gradual penetration have carried them over the whole world. I do not doubt that if we succeed in colonizing the moon, it will not be long before Shakespeare's plays are being acted there.

With the exception of the eighteen years between the closing of the theatres and their reopening at the Restoration, Shakespeare's plays have a continuous stage-history, enduring extraordinary transformations, rewritten to satisfy different dramatic conventions and different aesthetic ideals, with large cuts to make room for extra scenes, or for lavish spectacle, or to remove scenes, passages, or characters thought unworthy of our great national poet. During the last two centuries they have been translated into almost every possible language, often to the almost total destruction of their poetry, or played by English companies to audiences that can barely have followed what was being said. They have provided more plots for operas than the works of any other single writer, where, at least in some cases, the libretto has been at any rate based on the words of the play; but they have also been rendered into ballets, with no words spoken at all. They have been translated from their natural medium the stage onto the very different medium of the screen, in the cinema and now on television; and they have also been translated into a purely aural medium on the radio and on records. It is a most extraordinary and singular phenomenon, as Kenneth Muir reminded us at the Bicentennial Conference in Washington. [4]

When the theatres reopened at the Restoration the new playhouses were fundamentally different from the playhouses of Shakespeare's day. Behind the old platform stage, with its side entrances, there was now, framed by a proscenium arch, a room which accommodated movable scenery to be shunted on rollers from the wings, and also stage machinery. Both scenery that could be changed and machines by which characters could descend and ascend were legacies from the Stuart court masque, which combined poetry with spectacle of the most lavish and ingenious kind. It was the beginning of a process by which an aural appeal directed to the imagination of the audience was supplemented by, and to some degree replaced by, a visual appeal, spectacle coming to rival acting in its attraction to the spectator. It made much of Shakespeare's poetry seem redundant, for what need was there to describe what the scene-designer could present; and, as spectacular effects grew more and more ambitious, larger and larger cuts were necessary to make room for such displays or for additional scenes that would lend themselves to spectacular treatment. Eventually, the platform stage was sucked back through the proscenium arch. This destroyed the intimacy with which the Elizabethan actor directly addressed and involved his audience. It also provided a large stage on which crowds could be deployed in spectacular pageant-like scenes, a development that culminated at the beginning of the twentieth century in the productions of Beerbohm Tree, who created for the delight of the spectators scenes that Shakespeare could only describe, such as Cleopatra's first meeting with Antony at Cydnus and their reunion at Alexandria.

The appearance of the four Folio editions of Shakespeare's plays in the seventeenth century, the last two after the Restoration, witness to the existence from the beginning of people who wanted to read the plays as well as to see them acted, and the attempt to provide a better text for readers begins with Rowe in 1709. But throughout the eighteenth century and most of the nineteenth, when the foundations of the textual criticism of Shakespeare were laid and the plays were the inspiration of poets and the subject of great literary criticism, the stage went its own sweet way, treating the plays as scripts out of which plays could be made suited to the taste of the time, the current style of acting, and theatrical tradition. It is always a shock to recall the form in which the great Romantic critics of Shakespeare saw the great actors of their time playing: *King Lear* with no Fool, but with a romantic love-affair between Cordelia and Edgar, and a happy ending; *Richard III* with no Clarence or Queen Margaret, and with many minor characters removed to make room for additional soliloquies and villainies provided for the hero, the play becoming a one-man melodrama and a favourite vehicle for a star actor.

The greatest of the Restoration actors, Betterton, acted with immense dignity. He was acting in an age which saw the rise of the heroic play and in which the heroic poem was regarded as the noblest work of man. Poets still dreamed it might be possible to write one. Betterton was famous for his power of speaking verse, his art as an elocutionist being compared to the art of a great singer. The great actor of the mid-century, David Garrick, was his opposite. He electrified audiences by his naturalness and verve. His range can be judged by the fact that his two most famous roles were as Hamlet and as Abel Drugger, the pathetically gullible, little tobacconist in *The Alchemist*. It is fitting that a great novelist, who was also a dramatist, Fielding, has immortalized one of the great moments in Garrick's performance of Hamlet by his account of the terrifying effect of his reaction to the appearance of the Ghost on Tom Jones's simple companion, Partridge. With Fielding the rise of the novel begins, at first as a rival to the drama, but quickly to become the dominant literary form, eclipsing drama and powerfully affecting the art of acting. Towards the end of the eighteenth century there was a strong revival of the neoclassical ideal of great art as always general, and this was exemplified by the majestic Kemble, with his stately bearing and slow speech. It was a type of acting that suited the theatres of Drury Lane and Covent Garden when they were rebuilt at the turn of the century with huge auditoriums. Kemble's sister, Sarah Siddons, was more passionate than her brother and could be tender; but one thinks of her as the 'Tragic Muse', a Lady Macbeth, instinct with power. There were many stories of her impressive manner, and habit, like her brother, of dropping into blank verse on ordinary occasions. Scott, who greatly admired her, would mimic 'her tragic exclamation to a footboy' during dinner with him at Ashestiel: 'You've brought me water, boy, I asked for beer.' Another time, 'dining with a Provost of Edinburgh, she ejaculated, in answer to her host's apology for his *pièce de résistance*, "Beef cannot be too salt for me, my Lord!".'[5] Mr and Mrs Vincent Crummles may be thought of as deriving their acting style from Kemble and his sister.

Kemble's younger rival, Edmund Kean, was everything that Kemble was not, all fire and energy, flashing from one extreme of feeling to another, varying his pace, and employing long pauses. He was famous for his 'transitions' and made great use of facial expression to embody inner feeling. His greatest triumph was, perhaps, in *Othello*, when he played Othello and Iago on alternate nights, a feat Macready tried to emulate, but he failed in Iago and had to abandon the role. Kean created a famous piece of stage business in *Hamlet* that lasted on the stage certainly until Irving and, I believe, until Forbes-Robertson. It marks the appearance of the Hamlet of Romantic criticism on the stage, a more sensitive and a gentler figure than Johnson had conceived of. After his exit, crying 'To a nunnery, go!', Kean returned, and with a look of great tenderness and grief kissed Ophelia's hand. This action went behind the text to establish a presentation of Hamlet which reconciled his brutality to Ophelia on the only two occasions they appear together with his cry over her dead body: 'I loved Ophelia.' It anticipates the modern conception of the sub-text, which allows the actor to interpret a scene in the light of an overriding concept of the psychological consistency of a character against the plain sense of the text at that point. It also shows very interestingly the tendency to make a dramatic character awake the kind of sympathy which is called out by a character in a novel, when the novelist tells us that his real feelings are at variance with his behaviour, that his real self is different from the self he shows.

The great change that took place in the presentation of Shakespeare's plays in the nineteenth century, like the development of the historical novel and the popularity that grew through the century of paintings of historical subjects, was the result of the development of the historical imagination and of historical knowledge through the eighteenth century. The genius of Scott transformed historical romances and Gothic novels into novels that attempted to recreate the lives of men in past ages by blending invention with historical and antiquarian researches. The plays of Shakespeare came to seem to present the same mixture of invention with historical fact, and were treated as if they were the dramatic equivalent of *Ivanhoe*. As the century wore on, enormous pains were taken to give the plays their 'correct' historical setting, and programmes provided the audience with historical and archaeological notes by which they were given information of the conditions of life in ancient Britain to assist their appreciation of *Cymbeline*, and taught how to distinguish the Rome of *Coriolanus* from the Rome of *Julius Caesar*. Great care was taken to give a primitive British background to *King Lear*, which was helped by the depiction of Stonehenge on the backcloth. This 'mind exact for faultless fact' even went so far as the provision for little Mamillius in *The Winter's Tale*, set in ancient Sicily, of toys to play with copied exactly from archaic Greek figurines. Naturally, this desire for historical accuracy was particularly strong in the presentation of the sequence of English History Plays, and painters drawn to historical subjects from English history were attracted to scenes from Shakespeare with the characters correctly dressed according to the period of the action of the plays.

During the course of the nineteenth century, the texts were gradually improved by the discarding of old additions and alterations, although they were radically hacked to make time for scene-changing. It was towards the end of the century that the reaction set in against the sacrifice of Shakespeare's drama to spectacle. This was partly due to the resurgence of the drama; much more to the growth of modern scholarship in the universities and its consequence in the study of Shakespeare in schools, which led to the growth of an educated public. Bernard Shaw was a leader here. His attacks on Irving and Irving's successor,

Beerbohm Tree, still make wonderfully amusing reading. The pioneer in staging the plays was William Poel. He used a platform stage, with a small curtained inner stage, and a balcony above for scenes on castle walls, with actors dressed in Elizabethan costumes, and the whole lit from above with no footlights or spotlights. The actors were trained to 'speak the speech trippingly on the tongue'. Poel's highly austere conception of how Shakespeare should be presented could never have succeeded on the popular stage. His triumph was that he demonstrated the virtues of a platform stage and of letting the plays move swiftly onwards, instead of having them chopped up into short scenes to allow the scene-changers to do their work behind the front curtain. But he deprived his audience of any gratification of the visual sense. This was to be supplied by a new generation of scene-designers, the first and greatest being Gordon Craig, who broke with the attempt to represent the actual world by painted scenery, and instead provided imaginative and suggestive backgrounds which would express by forms and colours the spirit of the play. The full coming together of the study and the stage was achieved when Granville Barker, a distinguished playwright, with a record of brilliant productions of plays classical and modern, produced *The Winter's Tale* virtually uncut in 1912. It was played before curtains in exotically beautiful costumes on a stage with different levels. He followed it by *Twelfth Night* two months later, and, early in 1914, produced *A Midsummer Night's Dream*, in which his designer, Norman Wilkinson, presented the fairies all in gold, with their faces and limbs gilded to match their costumes.[6]

Granville Barker was not in the modern sense a director. He was a great producer. His whole aim was to educe the utmost from his actors by concentrating with them on their delivery of the words Shakespeare had written for them to speak. I once had the pleasure of sitting by John Gielgud at a small dinner-party, and asked him what it had been like to act with Granville Barker. He launched into a long description of being rehearsed for the final scene of *King Lear*, and of how Barker worked at the scene with him, not by analysis but by bringing to light significances in the lines.

He did this not only for his leading actors but for all the cast, however minor the roles were. Cathleen Nesbitt, who played Goneril, tells a story in her memoirs that illustrates this:

There was one actor who played a Captain, a practically non-existent part. He followed Lear on to the stage and had but one line to say after Lear's wonderful lines: 'Now she's gone for ever! Cordelia, Cordelia! Stay a little. Ha! What is't thou say'st? Her voice was ever soft, gentle, and low, an excellent thing in woman. I killed the slave that was a-hanging thee.' The Captain says, ''Tis true, my lord, he did.' The actor just said it, not ill or well, just said it. Barker called him aside and said quietly, 'That is an extremely important line. You must let the audience *feel* you have seen a miracle—you *have*—you are not accustomed to miracles—you are a rough soldier. "If it be man's work I'll do it" is about the only line you have. It has established your character and now you have seen with your own eyes a very old man, at the point of death, kill a man with his own hands, pick up a body—and a dead body is difficult to carry—and Miss Tandy is quite a tall woman. You have seen a thing that is not possible, yet you have seen it—your heart must beat faster when you say: '"Tis true, my lord, he did." It must be with awareness that almost stops Lear's rage for a second—he must *feel* you there and turn to *you*. "Did I not, fellow?"'[7]

One other thing was necessary to bring about what I regard as the classic period in the playing of Shakespeare. This had a humble beginning, just before the outbreak of war in 1914, when in a shabby music-hall in the Waterloo Road the Old Vic began its career of fifty years as a Shakespearean repertory theatre. Most of the great actors of the mid-century had their apprenticeship here. They were badly paid and hard worked. The theatre ran on a shoe-string under that wonderfully eccentric, benevolent despot, Lilian Baylis. She proved that lavish expenditure and elaborate stage-machinery were not necessary to the production of a Shakespearean play, and that a large and very mixed audience could respond with rapt attention to straightforward playing. Towards the end of its career the Old Vic became rather fashionable and the audience more sophisticated. When I was a schoolgirl and an undergraduate in the twenties the audience represented every level, social and intellectual. Many were obviously seeing a play they had no acquaintance with. It was one of the pleasures of going to overhear, in a hoarse whisper from the row behind, 'I think she must be walking in her sleep. Pass it along to Mum.' It was like being in the kind of mixed audience that Shakespeare wrote for.

By the classic period I mean the years from the early nineteen-twenties to 1960, when Shakespeare in the study and Shakespeare in the theatre came together. For many of the great productions I saw I have no idea who was the producer. I remember Gielgud's two Hamlets and the *Romeo and Juliet* in which he and Olivier exchanged the roles of Romeo and Mercutio and Peggy Ashcroft played Juliet to Edith Evans as the Nurse. I remember that the costumes were by a firm called Motley and were extremely beautiful. I do not remember, if indeed I ever knew, who produced Robeson in *Othello* with Peggy Ashcroft as an exquisite Desdemona. And in the fifties, during the period when Byam Shaw was producing at Stratford, nobody spoke of Byam Shaw's *Macbeth* or his *As You Like It*, but of Olivier's Macbeth, the greatest Macbeth I have seen, and of Peggy Ashcroft's 'heavenly Rosalind'. Byam Shaw, like Barker, did not direct the play; he produced fine acting from the whole cast. The audience were left free to respond to the play as it developed. One name does stand out for me from the period between the wars: that of Komisarjevsky whose productions at Stratford in the thirties shocked many. I saw his first production in England in 1927 when the Oxford University Dramatic Society invited him to produce *King Lear* as their winter play. The women's parts, as was usual at that time, were taken by professional actresses. The play was performed on a bare stage, broken by different levels, with what was then a new device, a cyclorama, at the back, over which during the storm scenes angry clouds drifted. The play was cut, but not too severely, and the storm scenes were run together; but there was no attempt to force an interpretation. It was presented in all its naked force. The young amateur actors spoke the lines well and had obviously benefited by acting in rehearsal with actresses of the stature of Dorothy Green as Goneril and

Martita Hunt as Regan. The Fool was John Fernald. I had not 'done' *King Lear* at school, and as soon as I heard it was to be the OUDS play I decided I would not read it before I went. Even with amateurs acting, Komisarjevsky's *King Lear* remains one of the great theatrical experiences of my life. In paying tribute to Oxford's enterprise in inviting him to come over from Paris, I must not forget to mention the achievements of the Marlowe Society at Cambridge, with George Rylands as their producer. The records made by the Marlowe Society are, as a whole, the finest recordings of Shakespeare's plays. Towards the end of the period I call classic the new Directors' Theatre was already appearing with Tyrone Guthrie's productions and, spectacularly, with Peter Brook's brilliant *Titus Andronicus* in 1955.

The Directors' Theatre has not divorced itself from the study. On the contrary, it is often very clearly dependent on interpretative readings of the plays derived from modern critics, most of them academics. Many of the younger directors have themselves read English at a university. Some have even taught it. Whereas at the height of the Victorian passion for historical realism and archaeological exactitude the audience were provided with information to help them to enjoy and appreciate the precision with which ancient Britain or the Sicily of the sixth century BC was presented to them on the stage, at Stratford today the expensive programmes are full of excerpts from whatever critics the director has based his reading of the play on. The audience, before the play begins, are given a little coaching on how they are to take what they are going to see. Even when this is not so, it is often quite obvious to those acquainted with modern Shakespearean criticism whose version of the play they are seeing performed. Who that had read Jan Kott's *Shakespeare Our Contemporary* could have failed to recognize that this was what Peter Brook's *King Lear* was presenting? This is something different from the adaptations, additions, and alterations, the variations in acting styles, and in presentation that Shakespeare's plays had endured through the centuries to make them stage-worthy and acceptable to changes in taste and outlook. But the Directors' Theatre has something in common with the

theatre from the Restoration until the close of the nineteenth century in its treatment of Shakespeare, although
its motive is different: its attitude to the text. This is only
partially to make it accord with modern acting styles,
modern theatrical methods of staging, and the tastes of the
theatre-going public. More often the plays are radically cut,
scenes added, and business introduced in flat contradiction
with words being spoken, or with the import of a scene, to
make the play accord with certain critical interpretations.[8]
The play is unified either by making everything that
happens subserve an overmastering theme, or by giving the
central character a simple consistent psychological motiv-
ation in all that he says or does. That it is found necessary to
treat the text so cavalierly casts great doubt on the validity
of the critical methods by which the interpretations foisted
onto the play on the stage have been reached. Whether the
search for a master theme, by the analysis of the imagery, or
by reference to Elizabethan philosophic, religious, or political conceptions, does justice to the fullness of the play;
and whether discoveries in what is called the sub-text—
what lurks between or beneath the lines spoken—or in the
imagery do justice to the vitality and vivacity of the
character's response to others, to his experience of his
world, and to his appeal to an audience, has always seemed
to me highly questionable. My experience of the Directors'
Theatre over the last ten to fifteen years has only confirmed
me in my scepticism.

It must at once be acknowledged that the style of
Shakespeare's plays presents great difficulties to a modern
actor, accustomed to the comparative inarticulacy and
understatement of most modern plays. Hyperbole and
lyricism, of which Shakespeare is so great a master, do not
come easily to him. It is remarkable how Gielgud has of
recent years adapted himself to acting in the style of the
plays of Pinter. It is a rather different matter for an actor
who has made his reputation acting in Pinter to change to
acting in Shakespeare. At the Washington Conference in
1976 Ian Richardson, describing how he approached a role,
said that, having been asked to play Richard II, he rang up
the 'Grand Old Man' to ask his advice. Gielgud replied: 'In

Shakespeare you have to see where the pauses come. (*Pause*)
In *Richard II* there are no pauses.' This is true. Regular
blank verse is a very rapid medium, much more rapid than
prose, since sense and stress help each other.[9] Richardson
then gave a brilliant demonstration of a few lines from the
play spoken in the modern naturalist manner, the pauses
leading to the bafflement of the hearers, who lost the sense
of the sentence while wondering what was coming next.
The slowness with which much of the verse is spoken today,
as if the speaker were groping his way towards a meaning, is
one reason why the plays have to be cut. They seem very
long even so, as if they might go on for ever. This
particularly applies to bawdy scenes and speeches, which
rarely suffer cutting. The words here have to be underlined
and accompanied by gestures so that no *double entendre* is
missed. Again, modern audiences are used to very vigorous,
even violent, action on films and on television, and to a good
deal of athleticism also. This also takes up time at the
expense of the words. It is nice to have a Hamlet and
Laertes who look capable of playing a long bout with the
foils, and to have Romeo, Mercutio, and Tybalt played by
athletic-looking young men. But in some recent productions
I have felt enough is enough, and longed for the actors to
stop the exhibition of their fencing skills and let the action
proceed. Battles are long drawn out and are very ferocious
and bloody. This also takes up a good deal of time. These
features of modern productions are the equivalent in their
effect on the text of scene-changing in the Victorian theatre.
They are there to satisfy our taste for a different kind of
realism. But these are minor cavils.

The most striking example of athleticism, permeating in
this case the whole play, was Peter Brook's *A Midsummer
Night's Dream*, set in what looked like a white-walled
gymnasium, in which the actors were turned into circus-
performers and gymnasts, swarming up ladders, flying on
ropes, standing on swings, juggling with spinning plates,
tossed and caught between a swinging Oberon and a
swinging Puck. I enormously enjoyed this evening and
found it wonderfully liberating and imaginative. The verse
was most beautifully spoken, rapidly, clearly, and musically.

The young lovers were teenagers and Helena looked and behaved just like the gawky, awkward one who gets left out. The mechanicals were in deadly earnest over their play and acted it with touching conviction, which made the court's reception of it seem less like condescending patronage and more like genuine enjoyment. At the end the performers ran down the aisles of the theatre with the audience stretching out their hands to shake hands as they passed in greeting and thanks. I put out mine with the others. I now know that I was too innocent, but I think the great majority of the audience were so too. I had not then read my Jan Kott, so I had no idea of what it was all supposed to be about until I read the Director's explanation of the interpretation he and the cast had arrived at in discussions and rehearsals. I had, of course, recognized that Theseus, Hippolyta, and Philostrate were doubling as Oberon, Titania, and Puck, and that Bottom, as he was carried to Titania's bower to the strains of Mendelssohn's Wedding March, had been provided with an ass's penis, and that there was a good deal of romping going on among the lovers. But I cannot deny my own experience in the theatre, where, like little David Copperfield reading Smollett, whatever harm there was in it, there was none for me: 'I knew nothing of it.' I had no idea that I was witnessing a sex-orgy, that Oberon was punishing his wife Titania by making her commit bestiality, or that, in the persons of Oberon and Titania, Theseus and Hippolyta were working out their own sexual problems, or any of the dreary absurdities and solemn nonsense with which Kott has smeared the play. The play, as performed, simply defeated, by the beauty of the language and the high spirits of the performers, the supposed meaning as far as I was concerned. Little was cut, the atmosphere of gaiety and magic was sustained, the intended implications of the doubling and some additional business could be passed over and I felt free to enjoy the play. I did not feel directed. Of Brook's *King Lear* I will say little. It has been finely dealt with by Maynard Mack.[10] By cutting of episodes, by the addition of business, by staging, costumes, and the direction of the leading actors, the audience was masterfully directed to accept Kott's interpretation of the play as Shakespeare's anticipation of Samuel Beckett's *End Game*. It was the most grievously reductive production of a great masterpiece I have ever seen.

In recent years there have been some total remakings of the plays by a process of taking them to pieces and reassembling the parts, as Marowitz did with *Hamlet* and *Macbeth*. This is a different process from what Davenant and Dryden employed when they made a new play, *The Enchanted Island*, out of *The Tempest*. Marowitz treats a play as if it were fragments of coloured glass set in a kaleidoscope which by shaking can be made to reveal different patterns. Both the deconstruction and the reconstruction are governed by the desire to discover alternative meanings and patterns in Shakespeare's plays and, needless to say, the patterns discovered are found to be relevant to today's concerns. I did not see either of these productions and speak only by report. More interesting than these way-out rehashings is the revival of the idea that Shakespeare can be improved by additional scenes as well as by cutting. In 1953 the Birmingham Repertory Company boldly staged the three parts of *Henry VI* on three successive nights and the production was brought to the Old Vic where I saw it. It was acted straight, with the minimum of the necessary hacking and hewing. The only liberty taken with the text was that at the close of the three plays Richard of Gloucester remained alone upon the stage, limped up to the throne his elder brother Edward IV had just vacated, and spoke the opening soliloquy of *Richard III*. I thought this wholly legitimate, as the close of the third part of *Henry VI* is not a real ending; it is only a pause in the ding-dong of Lancaster, York, Lancaster, York, which does not find its resolution until Bosworth Field. Even the first part played well and made me feel that poor Shakespeare was better than good anyone else. By the end of the third night I felt that my conviction, arrived at in the study, that in these three early plays Shakespeare reveals himself as already a master of dramatic tension and conflict, and of shaping a play, had been wholly justified. I still remember a beautiful performance by Jack May, who played the unhappy King. Some years later Stratford devoted a season to *The Wars of the Roses*, given on three successive nights. The great attraction was that Peggy Ashcroft played Margaret of Anjou from her first appearance as the young bride Suffolk woos for his master, the King, to her appearance as an old woman, the embodied memory of past outrages and wrongs, who against all probability haunts the court of Richard III. The three parts of *Henry VI* had to be drastically reduced to make two plays and were made intelligible by passages provided by the Director. Reduction was also necessary throughout the whole sequence by the amount of time needed for adequate representation of bloodshed and violence. (By the time *The Wars of the Roses* was staged Tillyard's view that the History Plays demonstrated the 'Tudor View of History', by which the anarchy of the Wars of the Roses led providentially to the establishment of the Tudor dynasty, had gone out of fashion in favour of a new view. This saw them as presenting a meaningless record of struggles for power, and of crimes, treacheries, and brutalities.) The same kind of treatment was later applied to *King John*, with rather fewer Grand Guignol effects. It had passages from *The Troublesome Reign* and Bale's *King Johan*, as well as from the Director's own pen, inserted into it.

I could continue for some time with accounts of the treatment that those favourite plays of our time, *Measure for Measure* and *Troilus and Cressida*, have received at the hands of various directors. But of all the productions I have seen in the last ten years John Barton's *Richard II* best illustrates the various means by which a Director can reduce a beautiful and moving play to a mere theatrical entertainment by imposing on it a simple, rigorous conception of the play's theme and structure, and a psychological interpretation of its central character. It had been announced that Richard Pasco and Ian Richardson were to exchange roles and the programme notes made clear how we were to look upon the play. We were told, with an expected reference to Kantorowicz's *The Two Bodies*, that 'Richard's journey from king to man is balanced by Bolingbroke's progress from a single to a twin-natured being. Both movements involve a gain and a loss. Each is in its own way tragic.' We were also told that some five hundred lines had been cut from the play and some twenty imported from *Henry IV*, Part I to fill out the part of Bolingbroke. We were not warned of the *coup de théâtre* at the close, which also added to Bolingbroke's part; for Richard's groom, wearing a monk's gown and cowl, at the close of his speeches, threw back his cowl to reveal himself as Bolingbroke. Although I suppose it can be said that to gain a crown is in some way tragic, since it imposes a role on the natural man, this is a very loose use of the term. But is it possible to regard Bolingbroke as he appears in this play, even with some additions from *Henry IV*, as in any way a tragic figure? He does not see himself as such or display himself to us as in a tragic situation. He shows no signs of fear or of any reluctance at the idea of ascending his cousin's throne. A tragic process of which the sufferer is wholly unaware, and a tragic figure who gives no expression to his sense of being in a tragic situation, is as impossible a conception as that of a 'mute inglorious Milton'. Whereas Shakespeare lavishes all his poetic resources at this stage of his career on presenting Richard's sense of his progress from a palace to the cell in which he is murdered as a tragic one.

As has been pointed out,[11] until the end of Act II, scene I all the memorable and moving poetry comes from the losers: from the widowed Duchess of Gloucester, from Mowbray and Bolingbroke condemned to exile from their native land, from the dying Gaunt. All of them reject comfort, and three of them forsee their own deaths. Richard in the first two acts is not poetical at all. He is royal, politic, ironic, insolent, selfish, irresponsible, and foolish. He is also tainted with the suspicion of complicity, if not with something worse, in the matter of his uncle Gloucester's murder. The change, which is astonishing, comes in a short scene between Busby and the Queen (II, ii, 1–41), when suddenly this cold and unattractive man is spoken of as 'my sweet Richard', and the Queen expresses in three rather tortuous speeches 'a nameless grief', an unaccountable sense of dread and foreboding. We know that her forebodings are to be justified, for at the close of the last scene we have heard the lords conspiring together, and the scene ended with the news that Bolingbroke was on his way back to England with 'eight tall ships' and 'three thousand men of war'. From this point onwards, with the exception of the Bishop of Carlisle's beautiful lines on Mowbray's death in exile and his prophecy of the horrors that will follow Bolingbroke's usurpation, and the unexpectedly moving account by York of Bolingbroke's entry into London, followed by Richard, all the poetry is Richard's.

In this production, to make Richard consistent psychologically, he was treated throughout as a role-player and a childishly theatrical one at that. And to make Bolingbroke balance him, he was made a role-player too. Both actors had to perform the difficult feat of acting persons who were only acting, and so not to be taken seriously. It is hardly surprising that all tragic feeling was lost, and that the poetry had to be played down.[12] We began with two actors looking at the prompt-book to decide which of them was to play which part. They held the crown between them, with the golden cloak of majesty hanging by. Having agreed, the Bolingbroke of the night dropped his hand, and the Richard, smiling, put on the robe and crown. It was an opening that at once gave the note of pure make-believe, in accordance with the fashionable belief that, as art is an illusion, the audience need to be reminded of this by the destruction of the illusion. The stage was bare, but at the back were two escalators joined by a bridge which they were able to move up and down. The opening scene was played straight. The first shock came in the second, when the Duchess of Gloucester emerged, but only so far as the waist, from a trap. She was holding a skull in her hand and appeared to be wearing some kind of shroud. It was difficult to decide whether she was a ghost rising from her husband's grave or a widow who had taken up residence in a charnel house. Either way, her position did not make for any very dramatic rendering of her encounter with Gaunt. For the next scene, in the lists at Coventry, no expense had been spared. Richard was lifted up high on a dais, Bolingbroke and Mowbray were riding on gaily caparisoned hobby-horses, wearing elaborate jousting helmets. Northumberland and his son were also on hobby-horses;

but theirs were black, as was their armour, and the horses were larger, so that when they discarded their mounts the Percies had to walk on small stilts. After all this expense it was a surprise to find the dying Gaunt unprovided even with a chair or any kind of robe. He lay on the floor clad in a kind of winceyette nightshirt, open to show his aged chest, and from this position did his best to do justice to the great speech on England. The king, when he arrived, had to sit on the floor by him, where, during his uncle's 'wholesome counsel', he displayed his inattention and childish incivility by sniffing and turning away with expressions of disgust at the smell of the dying man's breath.

I can only select some other moments. The bridge at the back was raised up to be the walls of Flint Castle, so that the great and moving moment when Richard deliberately descends to the base court—'base court where kings come down'—was rendered by his being borne slowly and passively down on an elevator. The Queen's ladies wore masks, and the Queen might well have done so for all the expression she showed on her doll-like face. The masked ladies were present and glided about the stage during the Queen's farewell to her husband. Anything that interfered with the idea that the basic theme of the play was the exchange of roles between Richard and Bolingbroke was thus avoided. In the deposition scene Richard did not dash the mirror to the ground to break it. He pushed the glass out, leaving the empty ring-frame on the floor. Bolingbroke picked it up, held it over Richard's head mockingly for a moment, then dropped it over his neck. This piece of symbolic business effectively destroyed the impact of Richard's wonderfully quick retort to Bolingbroke's contemptuous dismissal of his play-acting with the mirror. The empty ring was preserved for the final confrontation when Bolingbroke, disguised as Richard's groom, produced it and held it between his face and Richard's. Finally, at the close, Richard, who was in chains in his prison, was hoisted swiftly high up above the stage where he was shot to death by an arrow. He dangled there, like a poor puppet no longer animated by a puppet master, deprived of his one moment of glory when he dies like the son of the Black Prince.

Why was it I could accept Peter Brook's *A Midsummer Night's Dream*, full of theatrical tricks and inventions, as a great dramatic experience and could not tolerate this *Richard II*? The one was true to the whole spirit of the play, which is a revel and a fantasy ending with general happiness. The interpretation, of which I was hardly aware, was not continually pressed home and did not govern the handling of all the episodes of the night. Barton's production fought the whole time against the play to make it conform to a generalizing theme, derived from an abstract theory developed by medieval jurists. It fought also against the development of the hero's part from the moment he enters upon the course that leads to total loss, to make it conform to an overriding idea of his essential hollowness and childish posing.

Richard II is Shakespeare's first attempt to dramatize a story that tells of absolute disaster, complete defeat, the stripping away of all support, and ends with a man who was once a king alone in a prison cell where he is brutally murdered. The pity that 'renneth sone in gentle herte' had shown itself earlier in episodes in the first History Plays when persons, whether guilty of wicked deeds or not, when brought to terrible extremities, call for our pity: York taunted with the napkin stained with the blood of his little son by the savage Margaret, Margaret herself with her young son killed before her eyes, Constance lamenting her child's imprisonment. In *Richard II* the whole story that Shakespeare chose to dramatize told of loss and defeat, of a king 'fallen, fallen, fallen, fallen, fallen from his high estate'. Richard holds the centre throughout, and from the beginning of the third act he dominates the play by his swift intelligence, his irony, his power to grasp and expose the realities of the situation, and most of all by the power of the poetry with which Shakespeare endows him. At the moment of his greatest humiliation, the deposition scene, he makes Bolingbroke dance to his tune. Though powerless to maintain his right, he does not free his successor from the guilt of usurpation. He may appear to 'undo himself', but his conviction is that he cannot, and it is as a 'true king' that he makes his exit, having managed to evade, by the play with the mirror and the request, at the close, of one boon, the demand that he should read over his sins 'to satisfy the commons'. Shakespeare anticipated here the far more subtle demonstration he later gave in *Hamlet* of the power of weakness, the freedom that comes from having nothing to lose. Like all great tragic characters Richard dramatizes himself and his plight. Perhaps in this early play, wholly in poetry, Shakespeare appeals too strongly to our pity, does not give us those correcting voices that in his later tragedies prevent us from finding certain outcries or gestures excessive, or from reacting against tragic play-acting as unworthy of a mature man. When Lear play-acts by kneeling before Goneril with

> Dear daughter, I confess that I am old;
> Age is unnecessary; on my knees I beg
> That you'll vouchsafe me raiment, bed, and food,

Regan's horrible, icy rebuke keeps us firmly on Lear's side:

> Good sir, no more; these are unsightly tricks.

And when in the storm with a histrionic gesture Lear cries 'Off, off, you lendings! Come, unbutton here!', he is checked, as we are, by the Fool's 'Prithee, nuncle, be contented: 'tis a naughty night to swim in.' There are no such checks and adjustments in *Richard II*. Carlisle's advice after Richard's beautiful, mournful aria on the death of kings,

> My lord, wise men ne'er sit and wail their woes,
> But presently prevent the ways to wail,

is a piece of dramatic irony. We have heard in the previous scene what Richard is to be told now, the last blow that falls on him on his return to England: that his uncle York, the Regent, has gone to join the rebellion. He has no force left, no means of preventing 'the ways to wail'. His only power is the power to wail.

Richard's request for a mirror in the deposition scene enables him to indulge, some would say, in another piece of self-dramatization and self-pity. This may be so; but it is also a device for avoiding the intolerable demand that he

should read over and own his crimes and so justify what he
can never admit: that a king can be deposed. The game that
Bolingbroke played here with the frame of the mirror,
holding this hollow semblance of a crown over Richard's
head and then mockingly dropping it as a kind of noose onto
his neck, and the extreme emphasis he laid upon

> The shadow of your sorrow hath destroyed
> The shadow of your face,

drew attention away from the swift intelligence and power
of Richard's reply:

> Say that again.
> The shadow of my sorrow? Ha! let's see.
> 'Tis very true: my grief lies all within;
> And these external manners of laments
> Are merely shadows to the unseen grief
> That swells with silence in the tortur'd soul.
> There lies the substance; and I thank thee, king,
> For thy great bounty, that not only giv'st
> Me cause to wail, but teachest me the way
> How to lament the cause.

Richard's acceptance of Bolingbroke's contempt for his
shadow-play, and his turning it to his own advantage by his
ironic thanks for the correction, is the one point in the play
where the speaker of its most moving poetry, and I cannot
but believe that through him its author, recognizes that a
temperance is needed in exercising poetry's power to wail
and lament. But the tragic poet has no other means but
external manners, acts, and words by which he can express
what 'swells with silence in the tortured soul'.

When Shakespeare took up tragedy again and wrote the
great sequence of plays that begins with *Julius Caesar*, he
had acquired a temperance in using those moments when a
character by expressive action and impassioned poetry
dramatizes for us the substance of inward grief, so that they
become peaks of revelation in plays that hold much else.
But just as I cannot accept the notion of Hamlet and Othello
as deplorably self-conscious, I cannot accept the notion that
Shakespeare conceived of Richard II as a childishly self-
indulgent, sentimental play-actor. Up to the last years the

part has always been regarded as a great acting part, which, having seen great actors in the role, I believe it is. I wonder how many persons who saw the Pope, visiting his native country, stoop and kiss the soil of Poland thought of Richard returning to England from his Irish wars; and I wonder how many remembered with some amusement essays they had listened to in which Richard's gesture was censoriously dismissed as a piece of sentimental exhibitionism. And how many were surprized when the Pope repeated this gesture in every country he visited? He did it because he was conscious of his office. He is not only a Pole, but Christ's Vicar on earth and so a native of every country. Richard's act is more than an uprush of personal feeling. It is the action of one who regards himself as God's Deputy, being King by lawful succession. This sense that he is the true king never leaves him. It grows throughout the play as he loses all the appurtenances of royalty. As I said earlier, after all our close reading and reflection in the study we have to remember that the plays of Shakespeare are scripts for production and, if we do, we shall have to acknowledge certain fundamental simplicities. I used to find that going to the theatre took me back to these, as well as showing me subtleties I had missed. Now I most often come out saying at best 'How interesting', or feeling that I have been defrauded and given a stone for bread, presented with a kind of caricature, almost a comic-strip presentation. Nobody, I think, could have been stirred to any feelings of pity by this production of *Richard II*, nor to any sense of the individuality with which Shakespeare endowed the hero of his first full-length treatment of the great primitive theme of the fall from great place. It is true that he does not treat it with the power he gave it later; but the works of a great artist's early period have a freshness and beauty of their own, which is not to be undervalued by complaining that they have not the range and grandeur of the works of his maturity. There are relations between *Richard II* and *Hamlet* and between *Richard II* and *King Lear*, in the hero's 'antic disposition' in the one case and in the great image of royalty stripped down to beggary in the other. What made Peter Brook's *King Lear* so desolating an experience was the same thing as made me reject John Barton's *Richard II* as a wholly inadequate rendering of a beautiful play: that in neither was I presented with the spectacle of 'a sight most pitiful in the meanest wretch, past speaking of in a king', which because it is so great and primitive an image of total loss gathers up into it all our own losses and griefs. Why have we become so terrified of giving way to feeling and why are our actors and their directors so anxious not to elicit feeling from us? In the search for some kind of 'meta-play' the unique power of drama to engage, enlarge, and purify our sympathies is destroyed.

NOTES

1 *On Reading Shakespeare* (London, 1933), 30.
2 *Discoveries, Works*, ed. Herford and Simpson (Oxford, 1947), viii, 625, translated freely from Vives, *De Ratione Dicendi*.
3 'Shakespeare and the Stoicism of Seneca', *Selected Essays*, 139.
4 'The Singularity of Shakespeare', *Shakespeare Pattern of Excelling Nature*, ed. D. Bevington and J. L. Halio (Cranbury, New Jersey, and London, 1978), 66–77.
5 J. G. Lockhart in his *Life of Scott* (2 vols., 1848, i. 250) tells both stories. In the original version in seven volumes (1837–8) he gives only the first.
6 This rapid summary is much indebted to the excellent article on 'Shakespeare's Plays in Performance' by Charles H. Shattuck, Appendix A in the *Riverside Shakespeare* (Boston, 1974). I owe my knowledge of the provision of archaic toys for little Mamillius to the thesis of a former pupil, David Rittenhouse.
7 *A Little Love and Good Company* (London, 1975), 193.
8 The speed with which this can happen is remarkable. It was only in 1979 that Stanley Cavell in an article in *Daedalus* and in his book *The Claim of Reason* brooded over the non-problem of the state of Desdemona's wedding-sheets. By 1980 on the London stage we have had an Othello searching through dirty linen to the puzzlement of the unlearned audience.
9 See a lively discussion of Shakespeare's use of prose and verse by Bonamy Dobrée in *Histriophone: A Dialogue on Dramatic Diction* (Hogarth Essays, London, 1925) based on the contention that blank verse is much easier to say than the bulk of prose and is much more easily memorized.
10 See *'King Lear' in Our Time* (Berkeley, California, 1965). Mack criticizes the 'determination to rationalize, or unify according to a

particular plan what is not regular, nor rational, or not really unifiable on that plan.' (p. 29.) On 'sub-texts', he remarks that 'even in the most sensitive hands, their effect is to do the work that in poetic drama is properly the work of the audience's imagination, and thus make "entertainment" out of what should be participation in a ritual enactment of one's deepest experience.' (p. 41.)

11   See Lois Potter, 'The Antic Disposition of Richard II', *Shakespeare Survey*, No. 27, 33–41.

12   Lois Potter puts this admirably: 'To say that Richard is an actor giving a performance is irrelevant: all good dramatic parts allow actors to behave like actors. But to ask an actor to play the part of an actor giving an unconvincing performance is theatrical suicide. No one can possibly take any interest in the future history of a character shown to be as hollow as his crown. Fops are minor figures in drama and rightly so.'

Chapter IV

Readers and Reading

Kenneth Burke wrote that 'The main ideal of criticism, as I conceive it, is to use all that there is to use.'[1] It is an ideal no single critic is likely to achieve. Professor Morris Zapp, in David Lodge's novel *Changing Places*, whose ambition was to kill Jane Austen for ever as a subject of criticism or research by dealing with all and every subject that could possibly arise out of reading her novels, was plainly suffering from delusions of grandeur. Even if we were to modify the statement and say more modestly that a critic should use 'all that he can use', some qualification is needed. It sounds too like an invitation to provide massive batteries of quotations and references to substantiate every point, however slender the contribution it makes to the main object of the enterprise, which is to help a reader to read with more understanding and enjoyment. Some restraint is needed if the value of the text is not to be reduced by the attempt to set it within the context of the writer's total achievement, the circumstances of his life, and the events and concerns of the age in which it was written. This restraint is best provided by a continual refreshing of one's memory of the writer's own words, a continual revival of the experience of reading the work. The information that we have gathered then sinks into the background, enriching and colouring our response.

I am happy to call to my support here Professor Stanley Fish, who, in his study *John Skelton's Poetry*, published in 1965, wrote that 'while a completely satisfactory reading of a poem depends, in part, on the awareness of what we may call the fabric of history, there is always a danger ... that the poem will be lost in that fabric', and complained that 'since the Skelton "renaissance" of the thirties', his poetry had been 'absorbed by several disciplines. For some, the entire canon is a document in the history ... of Cardinal

Wolsey. . . . A less obviously misleading approach involves the identification of critical questions with the questions of "intellectual history". Does Skelton herald the English Renaissance, or is he the last medievalist?' Fish declared that 'a criticism which classifies on the basis of the history of ideas is necessarily superficial'; but he found the approach of the literary historian no less superficial: 'For ideas he substitutes conventions.' The poet is thus 'reduced to a manipulator of conventions'. He concluded:

If I am correct, the locus of a Skelton poem is the narrator's mind. . . . In the last analysis my quarrel is with the almost conspiratorial unwillingness to admit that Skelton is in any way involved in his own poetry. We are offered Skelton, the political propagandist; Skelton, the voice of his age; Skelton, the student of convention; but not Skelton, the man, as he confronts a collision between his ideal and an unwelcome reality in terms that are historically and personally unique. . . . Literary criticism is parasitical, and critics sometimes suppress an awareness of their dependence on a poet by implicitly denying his existence.[2]

Professor Fish concluded his first book by quoting C. S. Lewis on Skelton: 'He stands out of the streamy historical process, an unmistakeable individual, a man we have met.' And he added: 'I would like his friends who have read this book to feel they have met him again.'

We are all entitled to change our opinions; but Professor Fish's transformation in his next book, *Surprised by Sin : the Reader in Paradise Lost*, published only two years later, showed a startling shift of view. The 'locus' of the poem is no longer the narrator's mind. Instead, 'the poem's centre of reference is the reader who is also its subject'. We do not encounter Milton the man, except in one aspect: that of a teacher whose aim is 'to worry his reader, to force him to doubt the correctness of his responses' and who has a 'programme of reader harassment.'[3] The Milton who makes a brief appearance in the last pages of Professor Fish's earlier book as a poet who, unlike Skelton, had no lack of 'warmth and compassion', and had 'an ability, which links him with Chaucer, to understand the attractiveness of the human values which draw men from the worship of God and the maintenance of his order'[4] is transformed into a denigrator of human values. We are told that when Milton lists the great armies of literature, the intention is 'not in any way to magnify the strength of human armies, but to denigrate it'. There is a 'sneering tone', and one should hear 'the contempt in "mortal prowess"'.[5] I had always thought the intention here was to impress on us the strength and huge size of Satan's army, when compared with the great armies of epic and romance, just as I had never thought that a comparative destroyed all the value of its positive: that 'the better fortitude of patience and heroic martyrdom' made fortitude itself worthless. In his original preface to *Surprised by Sin*, Fish declared that his thesis was 'simply, that the uniqueness of the poem's theme—man's first disobedience and the fruit thereof—results in the reader's being simultaneously a participant in the action and a critic of his own performance'. But in 1971, in the preface to the paperback edition of the book, he told us that it was 'a certain timidity' that had led him to 'construct a special argument for *Paradise Lost*'; but that now, while he still regarded it as important 'to specify the peculiarly circular nature of the reader's response to this poem; . . . it is the reader's relationship to any poem (or play or novel or essay) that is, or should be, our concern'. At the beginning of the preface, Fish noted with some complacency that 'in the three years since this book was published the assumptions underlying its methodology have gained some currency. One hears more and more talk of "the reader", his responses, and his experiences.'

Emphasis on the importance of the experience of the reader has been a recurrent stress in the criticism of this century, beginning with I. A. Richards's *Principles of Literary Criticism* in 1924, followed two years later by *Science and Poetry*. The thesis, as first put forward, was radically unhistoric and anti-contextual, for Richards began by regarding poetry as purely expressive of feelings, moods, and attitudes. Its importance lay not in anything said, but in its power to evoke attitudes and emotions in the reader. What may be called 'the sense of a poem' does not matter much; the 'intellectual stream is fairly easy to follow; . . . it matters only as a *means*'. Assertions in poetry are 'pseudo-statements' and a 'pseudo-statement' is 'justified by its effect in releasing or organising our impulses and attitudes'. The weakness of the theory was amply demonstrated by the protocols of Richards's pupils, many of them very clever young people, which he printed in *Practical Criticism* in 1929. It was clear that they found the 'intellectual stream' far from easy to follow when presented with no information, not even the name of the author. All the same, Richards was laying stress on something that much of the reader-orientated criticism of today seems to neglect: that poetry evokes very powerful emotional responses and very deeply engages our feelings: whether it praises and celebrates, or laments and mourns, or persuades and argues, or expresses scorn, contempt, or rage, or just gaiety and lightness of heart. And it does so not merely through the significances of words in their denotations and connotations, and in their grammatical and syntactical relations, and through figures of thought (tropes), but also in a play of sounds of all kinds—alliteration, rhyme, assonance, repetitions and echoes—and most of all in the pace and pulse of the verse. Nobody could speak about poetry with Richards, or hear him read it, without being moved by the depth of his personal response. In spite of the polite irony of Eliot's criticism of his advice on how to prepare oneself for reading a poem, Richards never lost his feeling that there was about poetry something of the sacred.[6]

Richards's doctrine was attacked by Wimsatt and Beardsley as 'the affective fallacy', for 'confusing a poem and its results (what it *is* and what it *does*)'. It begins, they declared, 'by trying to derive the standards of criticism from the psychological effects of the poem and ends in impressionism and relativism. The outcome . . . is that the poem itself, as an object of specifically critical judgment, tends to disappear.' In his 1971 preface Fish declared that he embraced and, indeed, went beyond the affective fallacy thus defined, for to make the poem itself disappear as an object 'exactly' defined his intention. At first sight it would seem that he also embraced the second of Wimsatt's famous fallacies, the 'intentional fallacy'. Both in *Surprised by Sin* and its successor, *Self-Consuming Artifacts*, published five years after, we are constantly being told what the author 'intends'. But the intentions of Milton and of the authors handled in *Self-Consuming Artifacts* are not established by what they themselves said. They are again discovered in what the poem or prose work *does* to the reader, and what it *does* is discovered by Fish's theory about the process of reading, which is the basis of his interpretative method. 'Throughout *Paradise Lost*', we are told,

Milton relies on the operation of three truths so obvious that many critics fail to take them into account: (1) The reading experience takes place in time, that is, we necessarily read one word after another; (2) the childish habit of moving the eyes along a page and back again is never really abandoned although in maturity the movement is more mental than physical, and defies measurement; therefore the line as a unit is a resting place even when rhyme is absent; (3) a mind asked to order a succession of rapidly given bits of detail (mental or physical) seizes on the simplest scheme of organisation which offers itself.[7]

I imagine we would all agree that words, like music, move in time. And that we would also agree that we read words in sequence. And further that in reading complex sentences our expectations as to how the meaning will develop are often fulfilled in unexpected ways. This last is one of the major pleasures of reading a work of literature. But I am not prepared to accept as a truth that the process of reading a sentence involves not only expectations but actual surmises about how it will develop, and that these (although no reader is conscious of them and, if they do exist, we are told, they are immediately suppressed) are still 'available' somehow to an 'attentive reader' and qualify or 'undercut' the reading finally arrived at. This last supposed truth is proved by artificially slowing down the reading process to bring these supposed mental 'events' before our analytical attention. 'It is', writes Fish, 'as if a slow-motion camera with an automatic stop action effect were recording our linguistic experiences and presenting them to us for viewing.'[8] It sounds impressively scientific, as if we were in a language laboratory. But the analogy is a false one. No athlete is himself asked to perform his feats in slow motion and to stop in mid-air with both feet off the ground while he considers possible next movements. It is the camera that slows down its record of his actual performance and the film, not the high-jumper, that is stopped at the split second when he is in mid-air. I do not doubt for a moment that Fish can persuade his students that this is how they really read. Students are highly suggestible. If their teacher is addicted to Freudian interpretation they will happily discover the primal scene in poem after poem. I am sure that Fish's pupils busily provide him with evidence of what the poem 'does to them' when read by this 'stop and go' method, in the same way as the patients of the 'displaced (and, surely, deranged)' celebrity in *Lolita* could be made to believe that they had witnessed their own conceptions.

The immense complexity of mental processes, including the power of the human mind to cognize, to understand what is said or what is read, takes place in time, the process by which the past incessantly moves into the future. To concentrate on our power to expect while ignoring our power to retain is to destroy the enchainment of past and future in mental experience. We are told more than once that 'the reader' making his way by the 'stop and go' method, as he fumbles his way through a long sentence, has forgotten that it began with a negative. Who is this reader, who cannot carry anything forward, but can only attempt to surmise how the sentence will go on in an artificially produced and spurious present? As he gropes his way forward he has also not retained in mind the sentence that goes before, which might help him not to find the one he is engaged with so unsettling and baffling.

Fish owns that 'the reader' is a construct, Milton's 'fit reader', or in his own preferred term, 'the informed reader'. He must possess 'linguistic competence', a term that has a defined meaning in linguistics, and in addition, he must possess 'literary competence' a term that nobody has so far succeeded in defining. The 'informed reader' will bring to his experience of reading 'a matrix of political, cultural, and literary determinants' appropriate to the work he is reading. This last qualification follows on a declaration that the method is 'radically historical'. For a moment one wonders whether Fish is really an old-fashioned 'history of ideas' man, fashionably disguised. He does indeed call upon a considerable amount of quotation from contemporary writers, and gives ample references to recent scholarly studies. But this documentation does not provide historical evidence to confirm, extend, enrich, or call in question the reader's response to the text. It buttresses and supports a thesis, adumbrated in his study of *Paradise Lost*, and extended to include all literature in *Self-Consuming Artifacts*: that there are two opposed kinds of literary presentation. There is the rhetorical, which mirrors and presents 'for approval the opinions its readers already hold', and flatters the reader by telling him 'that what he has always thought about the world is true and that the *ways* of his thinking are sufficient'; and there is the 'dialectical', which is 'disturbing', requiring of its readers 'a searching and rigorous scrutiny of everything they believe in and live by'. The aim of the dialectical method is to change its readers, and move them from 'the natural way of discursive, or rational, understanding', which operates by distinguishing entities, to a mode that is 'antidiscursive and anti-rational; rather than distinguishing, it resolves, and in the world it delivers the lines of demarcation between places and things fade in the light of an all-embracing unity'.[9] The work made is thus 'Self-Consuming' in two senses. It ends by destroying its own rational structure and it destroys the self of the reader, if he has submitted to this purging and humiliating process.

In *Surprised by Sin* Fish postulated a reader's pause at the end of a line, and he was willing to concede that there was a correct reading that, on going back and re-reading the sentence, the reader would find. His theory there was that the wrong surmises as to how the sentence would proceed remained as part of the reading experience and coloured or qualified the sense finally arrived at. In *Self-Consuming Artifacts*, the works considered, except for Herbert's *The Temple*, are in prose. Closures are thus completely arbitrary. Whereas one might complain that in his treatment of *Paradise Lost* Fish selected only a few passages to display his 'stop and go' method, the passages chosen were in the main key passages, which had been the subject of much discussion, and on which critics had fastened in their discussions of the poem. In taking a sentence out of a long sermon by Donne, or out of a work of the length of *The Anatomy of Melancholy*, and asking us to accept it as paradigmatic of the whole and 'spectacularly self-consuming', Fish is like a man trying to sell a house by showing a brick.

A spectacular example of taking words out of their immediate context is Fish's statement that no one after the Restoration 'is willing to say, with Donne, that he intends "to trouble the understanding, to displace, and to discompose, and disorder the judgement"'.[10] I could not believe that Donne could ever in his sermons have given expression to such an intention, and on looking at the reference provided, I saw that he did not. Donne was preaching on the text 'Follow me and I will make you fishers of men.' He contrasts the plainness of Christ's injunction to 'weake men' with 'the Way of Rhetorique in working upon weake men', which is 'first to trouble the understanding, to displace, and to discompose, and disorder the judgement, to smother and bury in it, or to empty it of former apprehensions and opinions, and to shake that beliefe, with which it had possessed itself before, and then when it is thus melted, to powre it into new molds, when it is thus mollified, to stamp and imprint new formes, new images, new opinions in it.'[11] Donne's description of a sophist's use of rhetoric here is curiously like Fish's description of the way of dialectic; but, far from expression his own intention as a preacher, Donne is condemning such methods of persuasion.

Professor Fish relies heavily throughout his book on three lines taken from a poem by George Herbert, and particularly on the last line:

> We say amisse,
> This or that is:
> Thy word is all, if we could spell.

I had no need to look up the reference here, as I know this poem, 'The Flower', by heart; but even if I had not known the context of the lines I should have known that the explanation of their meaning could not possibly have been right. 'The point of doctrine', we are told, 'is, of course, a seventeenth-century commonplace':

> If God is all, the claims of other entities to a separate existence, including the claims of the speakers and readers of these poems, must be relinquished. That is, the insight that God's word is all is *self*-destructive, since acquiring it involves abandoning the perceptual and conceptual categories within which the self moves and by means of which it separately exists. To stop saying amiss is not only to stop distinguishing 'this' from 'that', but to stop distinguishing oneself from God, and finally to stop, to cease to be. Learning to 'spell' in these terms is a self-diminishing action in the course of which the individual lets go, one by one, of all the ways of thinking, seeing, and saying that sustain the illusion of his independence, until finally he is absorbed into the deity whose omnipresence he has acknowledged.[12]

This is not a doctrine that I have met with in any seventeenth-century Protestant, although it bears some kind of resemblance to the Quietism of Mme Guyon in France, which verges on Pantheism. To speak of man becoming unable to distinguish himself from God and being finally absorbed into the deity is totally unscriptural. To stop saying amiss is not to stop distinguishing one thing from another, but to stop ascribing independent and unchanging being to any created thing, for only God can truly say 'I am'.[13] In the stanza which the lines conclude and in the poem Herbert wrote, the contrast is between the unchanging word, command, or ordinance of God, which 'endureth for ever' and is 'true from everlasting' and the mutability of the natural world of which man is a part.

> These are thy wonders, Lord of power,
> Killing and quickning, bringing down to hell
> And up to heaven in an houre;
> Making a chiming of a passing-bell.
> We say amisse,
> This or that is:
> Thy word is all, if we could spell.

The word 'quickning' recalls at once the psalm from which I have just quoted, Psalm 119, where the words 'quicken me according to thy word', occur three times (vv. 25, 107, 154), and the verb 'quicken' occurs on seven further occasions.[14] Herbert does not 'collapse' all categories when he employs the favourite seventeenth-century metaphor which relates the life of man to the growth and decay of plants, and their dependence on the quickening powers of sun and rain, any more than Donne ever said, as a preacher, that his intention was 'to trouble the understanding'.

Self-Consuming Artifacts opens with a presentation of the *Phaedrus* of Plato as the archetypal self-consuming artifact, which is followed by a discussion of the fourth book of Augustine's *De Doctrina Christiana* to discover what a sermon 'faithful to the spirit of *On Christian Doctrine* would be'. While nobody would deny the strongly Platonic cast of Augustine's thought, an attempt to bring together a Platonic dialogue and a Christian sermon as ways of teaching ignores the profound difference between a philosophic treatise, which appeals to the understanding, and a Christian sermon, which is directed not only to the understanding but also to the heart and conscience. Further, the Christian preacher's main duty is to open the Scriptures. He is not following where an argument leads, but expounding a text, and applying it to the circumstances in which men live in this world. When Fish speaks of the 'Christian–Platonic' memory, he is, to use his own word, 'collapsing' two fundamentally different things: a theory of knowledge and the Christian belief that God has spoken to men, that he has acted in and through human history, and, supremely, that he has revealed himself in the life and death of Jesus, the Christ. Donne makes the distinction clear in a passage that Fish quotes. '*Plato* plac'd *all learning* in the memory; wee may place *all Religion* in the memory too. All knowledge, that seems new today, says *Plato*, is but a remembring of *that*, which your soul knew before. All instruction, which we can give you today, is but the remembring you of the mercies of God, which have been *new every morning*.'[15] The Christian must call constantly to memory both the wonderful works of God as recorded in Scripture and the mercies he has received in his own individual life: events in human history and the events of his personal history.

Donne's last sermon, *Deaths Duell*, is handled at length by Fish as his first example of a 'self-consuming artifact' employing the 'dialectical' as opposed to the 'rhetorical' mode of presentation. Although not one of Donne's finest sermons, it is, perhaps, the most famous on account of its occasion, since it was preached by a visibly dying man. It touches on many of the themes that had preoccupied Donne as a preacher. Published soon after his death, it was given a rather inappropriate title taken from another man's work,[16] but justly subtitled *A Consolation to the Soule, against the dying Life, and living Death of the Body*. Donne's conception of his office was to be 'the Minister and Dispenser of the Word of God' and he saw this as a ministry of consolation:

Who but my selfe can conceive the sweetnesse of that salutation, when the Spirit of God sayes to me in a morning, Go forth to day and preach, and preach consolation, preach peace, preach mercy, And spare my people, spare that people whom I have redeemed with my precious Blood, and be not angry with them for ever; Do not wound them, doe not grinde them, do not astonish them with the bitternesse, with the heavinesse, with the sharpnesse, with the consternation of my judgements. *David* proposes to himselfe, that he would *Sing of mercy, and of judgement*; but it is of mercy first; and not of judgement at all, otherwise then it will come into a song, as joy and consolation is compatible with it. . . .

What a Coronation is our taking of Orders, by which God makes us a Royall Priesthood? And what an inthronization is the coming up into a Pulpit, where God invests his servants with his Ordinance, as with a Cloud, and then presses that Cloud with a *Vae si non* . . . woe be unto thee, if thou doe not preach, and then enables him to preach peace, mercy, consolation, to the whole Congregation. That God should appeare in a Cloud, upon the Mercy Seat, as he promises *Moses* he will doe, That from so poore a man as stands here, wrapped up in clouds of infirmity, and in clouds of iniquity, God should drop raine, poure downe his dew, and sweeten that dew with his honey, and crust that honied dew into Manna, and multiply that Manna into Gomers, and fill those Gomers every day, and give every particular man his Gomer, give every soule in the Congregation, consolation by me.[17]

I have given a passage of some length to pass from Donne's stress on the preacher's duty to console to his attitude to

rhetoric, since the passage is highly rhetorical. Far from
distrusting rhetoric as appealing to the senses and to the
carnal in man, Donne defended rhetoric and eloquence in
sermons by the example of Scripture:

Religion is a serious thing, but not a sullen; Religious preaching is
a grave exercise, but not a sordid, not a barbarous, not a
negligent. There are not so eloquent books in the world, as the
Scriptures: Accept those names of Tropes and Figures, which
the Grammarians and Rhetoricians put upon us, and we may
be bold to say, that in all their Authors, Greek and Latin, we
cannot finde so high, and so lively examples, of those Tropes,
and those Figures, as we may in the Scriptures: whatsoever
hath justly delighted any man in any mans writings, is exceeded in the Scriptures. . . . So the Holy Ghost hath spoken
in those Instruments, whom he chose for the penning of the
Scriptures, and so he would in those he sends for the preaching
thereof. [18]

And in a famous sentence which combines his great theme
of God's mercy and his mode of communicating his sense of
it, he said: 'No metaphor, no comparison is too high, none
too low, too trivial, to imprint in you a sense of Gods
everlasting goodnesse towards you.' [19]

As well as commending and using rhetoric, which appeals
to the passions and emotions, Donne commends reason:
'Reason is our Soules left hand, Faith her right,' he wrote
as a poet, and he frequently echoes this commonplace in his
sermons. 'Mysteries of Religion are not the less believ'd and
embrac'd by Faith, because they are presented, and induc'd,
and apprehended by Reason', he said in an early sermon,
and in his first Christmas sermon as Dean of Paul's, he
declared: 'For let no man thinke that *God* hath given
him so much ease here, as to save him by believing he
knoweth not what, or why. *Knowledge* cannot save us, but
we cannot be saved without Knowledge; Faith is not on this
side Knowledge, but beyond it; we must necessarily come
to *Knowledge* first, though we must not stay at it, when we
are come thither.' [20] And he went on to speak of the light of
reason, 'thy faint and dimme knowledge of God, that riseth
out of this light of nature' as leading to a 'light of faith'. He

recurred to the same topic in a later Easter sermon, speaking of 'the light of naturall Reason, *which*, without all question, *enlightneth every man that comes into the world'* and adding 'yet have we light enough to see God by that light, in the Theatre of Nature, and in the glasse of Creatures'.[21] I am bringing my knowledge of Donne's sermons generally to bear on the reading of the sermon Fish has chosen: for my reading of Donne's sermons makes me think it unlikely that he would in preaching his last sermon be occupied in creating sentences that are 'an exercise in futility', or 'literally impossible to follow', putting forward a plan for his sermon, only to undermine and subvert it, and end by depriving his hearers of any initiative of 'both reason and will'. The patterns Fish finds in *Deaths Duell* 'constitute' he tells us, 'a radical subversion not only of the sermon's pretensions, but of the pretensions of those who are prepared (or so they think) to understand it and to exit from it with a portable truth'.[22] I am prepared to say I understand it and that I do not believe that the hearers in 1631 went away uninstructed or unmoved, having experienced what today we would call a 'happening' rather than what they had come to hear: an exposition of the word of God.

Fish begins his discussion by pulling out a plum, a single sentence, which he displays to us as 'spectacularly self-consuming'. He manages to make it so by ignoring a comment Donne himself makes later in the sermon to illustrate a point; that 'the first part of a sentence peeces well with the last, and never respects, never harkens after the *parenthesis* that comes betweene'. In the 'logic of experience' which he contrasts with 'the logic of syntax', Fish is thrown off course by finding the 'so' that he was expecting to follow on an opening 'Therefore as', occurring in a parenthesis and not once but twice. He finds that these 'so's' of the parenthesis are subversive of the expected 'so' of the second part of the main sentence, making the whole sentence meaningless. The sentence thus arbitrarily extracted from its context, sums up a long passage that might seem a digression, and its 'Therefore' refers back to this. It leads as a bridge directly to a characteristic message of comfort and consolation to troubled souls. It is not meaning-less, as I hope to show, in its context.

Having successfully misread his chosen sentence, Fish turns to the plan that Donne, in his usual fashion, lays down for his sermon. He takes for his text the second half of a verse from Psalm 68, of which he gives two versions: 'And unto God the Lord belong the issues of death, i.e. from death'. 'The issues of death' is the reading of the Geneva Bible; 'our translation', as Donne calls the King James Bible, has 'from death'. Donne will also refer to the Vulgate, which has '*exitus mortis*'. He begins his sermon: 'Buildings stand by the benefit of their *foundations* . . . of their *butteresses* . . . and of their *contignations*' [that is, what binds them together].

The body of our building is in the former part of this verse; It is this, hee that *is our God* is the *God of salvation*; *ad salutes*, of salvations in the plurall, so it is in the originall; the God that gives us spirituall and temporal salvation too. But of this *building*, the *foundation*, the *butteresses*, the *contignations* are in this part of the *verse*, which constitutes *our text*, and in the three divers *acceptations* of the words among our expositors, *Unto God the Lord belong the issues of death*.

'What is provided here', comments Fish, 'is, literally, a building or floor plan whose rooms are to be filled and furnished as we listen.'[23] On the contrary, what we have been told we are going to hear about is the foundation, buttresses, and contignations by which a building stands. The building is the first half of the verse: 'He that is our God is the God of salvation.' Why, you may ask, does Professor Fish talk about rooms 'to be filled and furnished' and complain in his discussion of the sermon that we never seem to get out of one room into another? He has read and been justly impressed by Frances Yates's admirable study *The Art of Memory*, where he has learnt that 'the commonest . . . type of mnemonic place system used was the architectural type'. Without in any way denying the value of Dr Yates's work, it is completely irrelevant here, unless we are to assume that all seventeenth-century hearers of the word 'building' assumed automatically that they were now going to hear about rooms and their furniture.

Having thus established that he is taking the half verse he has chosen for his text as supporting the generalization of the first half, Donne proceeds to split his text and tell his hearers what will be the three heads of his sermon. These are to be taken from three ways of taking the text. The first, the most obvious interpretation of the words, is that God delivers us *from* death, gives us *liberatio a morte*; the second that he gives us a deliverance in the hour of our own death, *liberatio in morte*; the third, which is Augustine's interpretation of *exitus mortis*, is that he gives us deliverance through death, *liberatio per mortem*, through the death of Christ. And he sums up the sermon he is about to preach by telling us how we should 'looke upon these words; *First*, as the *God* of *power*, the *Almighty Father* rescues his servants from the jawes of death: *And then*, as the *God* of *mercy*, the glorious *Sonne* rescued us, by taking upon himselfe this *issue of death: And then* betweene these two as the *God* of *comfort*, the *Holy Ghost* rescues us from all discomfort by his blessed impressions before hand, that what manner of death soever be ordeined for us, yet this *exitus mortis* shall bee *introitus in vitam*, our *issue in death*, shall be an *entrance into everlasting life*.' The sermon exactly follows this outline given at the beginning. There has never been any suggestion that we are going to pass from room to room of a building to arouse an expectation in the hearers that the sermon then continually frustrates. The belief that our God is the God of all salvations is to be strengthened by declaring how he saves in what men find most fearful. In many of his love-poems Donne wrote of parting as the great test of love: death in all its manifestations is the great challenge to faith. The text, which sounds through the sermon, like a refrain in a poem, or a motif in music, is used as a key to unlock the Scriptures, as other texts are brought to bear upon it, to reveal not some particular doctrine but the revelation contained within the word of God, who has shown himself as a God of Power, of Comfort, and of Mercy: Creator, Preserver, and Redeemer.

Let me leave the art of memory and not touch upon the *topos* of the seven ages of man, which we are told that Donne also 'subverts', and move to what Michelin Guides call *un peu d'histoire*. The sermon was preached on 25 February 1631. It should have been preached on 12 February, the first Friday in Lent, Donne's 'old constant day' to preach before the King in the chapel at Whitehall. Donne took orders on 23 January 1615, at the age for forty-two, and was almost at once appointed as one of the royal chaplains, with an obligation to preach at Court on the first Friday in Lent and on a day in April. As a favourite preacher of both James and Charles, Donne preached before them on other occasions; but these were his days of obligation. Lent is the season of preparation for the feast of Easter and it culminates on Good Friday. 'He that will dy with Christ upon Good-Friday must hear his own bell toll all Lent. . . . We begin to hear Christs bell toll now, and is not our bell in the chime?'[24] So Donne had begun his Lenten sermon in 1628. Now, three years later, he knew the bell would very soon be tolling for him.

Donne had been taken ill while staying with his daughter and her second husband in Essex in September 1630 and in November he had to decline an invitation to preach the Gunpowder Plot sermon. He was too unwell to preach the Christmas sermon at St. Paul's and in mid-December he made his will, a sign he knew his end was near. He had hoped to return to the Deanery to preach on 2 February, Candlemas Day, at St. Paul's, and at Whitehall on 12 February. There is no evidence that he preached at St. Paul's and the effort of preaching in that huge cathedral would probably have been beyond his strength. His friends tried to dissuade him from fulfilling his obligation to preach at Court, but he 'passionately denied their requests', although he had to postpone the date. Just over four weeks after he had preached *Deaths Duell*, on 31 March 1631, he died. The sermon was published, undoubtedly by his instructions, with an engraving of a portrait of him in his shroud as frontispiece.

There was almost certainly another reason beside his illness that kept Donne so long in Essex and made him write to a friend in late October that, although London would be good for his recovery, 'the very going would endanger me'. Five years before, in 1625, London had been visited by the worst outbreak of the plague since the Black Death of 1349. It was always referred to as the Great Plague, until its horrors were eclipsed by the Plague of 1665. In September 1630, after only five years, it seemed as if the plague were returning. The bills of mortality began to rise ominously in September, and mounted frighteningly through October and November. It was only by the end of December that it was clear that the danger had passed.[25] Many preachers had improved the occasion after the Great Plague to preach harshly to the wretched survivors on God's judgement for sin. George Wither wrote a long poem, *Britain's Remembrancer*, printed at his own expense in 1628, which combined denunciation of the sins of others with a note of satisfaction at his own virtue in not fleeing the city, as others had, and at his survival. Donne, who had been ill in the summer of 1625, was staying with his friend Magdalen Herbert at Chelsea when the 'plaguy bills' began to shoot up, and he remained with her as things grew worse, and refugees fleeing from London encamped at Chelsea in a kind of quarantine. He was able to return to preach his usual Christmas sermon at St. Paul's, and three weeks later he preached to his parishioners at St. Dunstan's a moving sermon on the text 'For there was not a house where there was not one dead'. Here, while recalling the dreadful scenes his hearers had witnessed, and speaking of the griefs of those recently bereaved, he did not speak of the visitation of the plague as a judgement for sin, but offered them the consolations of religion.

In preaching *Deaths Duell*, Donne was said to have preached his own funeral sermon; but *Deaths Duell* is not a funeral sermon, which is a commemoration of a dead person, including an account of his or her life, and a eulogy. Rather Donne's sermon was a *Praeparatio ad Mortem*. He was sharing with his listeners his own preparation for his impending death, generalizing from his own experience of the harshness of life, the facts of birth and sickness and the pains and agonies of death, from which men and women of earlier ages were not shielded as we are in the more prosperous parts of the world, and from his own experience of years of disappointment, poverty, and failure, and of the losses he had suffered. The very long first part begins with our deliverance from death in the womb: the gift of life itself. Fish's comment here that 'the effective agent is not time but God' ignores the terrible incidence of miscarriages and still births in earlier ages than ours, which made the safe delivery of a child from the womb seem more a mercy than something in the course of nature. Donne's own beloved wife had died in 1617 of a fever after giving birth to a still-born child, buried with her. Five years before that, when Donne was abroad, having unwillingly left his wife pregnant, he is reported to have seen a vision of her with a dead child in her arms at the very time she was delivered of a still-born child. The sermon goes on to survey the course of human life as a long process of dying, as youth passes into age, and ends with our deliverance from a dying life by the dissolution of the union of soul and body that makes man, and with the corruption of the body after death, which it was Christ's prerogative alone not to suffer. Then the sermon takes a strange turn in which Donne apparently goes off the straight road to indulge in some destructive criticism of reasons that might be brought forward to explain why the body of Christ was spared corruption. This, Donne declares is a Mystery of Religion, and he goes on: 'We looke no further for *causes* or *reasons* in the *mysteries of religion*, but to the *will* and pleasure of God. . . . Christs body did *not see corruption*, therefore, because *God* had *decreed* it shold not. The humble soule (and onely the humble soule is the religious soule) rests himselfe upon *Gods* purposes, and his decrees; but then, it is upon those purposes, and decrees of *God*, which he hath declared and manifested; not such as are *conceived* and imagined in ourselves. . . .' God's decree and purpose was declared in the words from Psalm 16 which Peter at Jerusalem and Paul at Antioch cited when preaching the Resurrection: 'thou wilt not suffer thy holy one to see corruption'. It was also manifested in its execution, when he raised Christ from the dead on the third day. And so we come to the sentence that Professor Fish picked out at the beginning of his discussion as 'an exercise in futility': 'And therfore as the *Mysteries* of our *Religion* are *not* the *objects of our reason*, but *by faith we rest* on *Gods decree* and purpose, (It is so, o *God*, because it is *thy will*, it should be so) so *Gods decrees* are ever to be considered in the *manifestation* thereof.' Donne in his last sermon is reverting to a theme that runs through his sermons. He is, for the last time, speaking to comfort 'diffident men', Mr Fearings; for, as he said more than once, he had met with more men that were diffident and dejected than with men who were presuming, more that doubted their salvation than presumed upon it. The word 'decree' is the clue. He is speaking in rebuke of the 'doctrine men', who spoke as if they had access to the secret, eternal counsels of God, those 'decrees of reprobation, decrees of condemnation' that preceded the decrees of creation.[26] He concludes his digression by declaring that 'All *manifestation* is either in the *word* of *God*, or in the *execution* of the *decree*; And when these two concur and meete, it is the strongest *demonstration* that can be'. And then, movingly, he slips into the first person singular: 'when therefore I finde those *markes* of *adoption* and *spiritual filiation*, which are delivered in the *word* of *God*, to be upon me, when I finde that reall *execution* of his *good purpose* upon me, as that *actually* I doe *live* under the *obedience*, and under the conditions which are *evidences* of *adoption* and *spirituall filiation*; then, and so long as I see these *markes* and live so, I may safely comfort myself in a *holy certitude* and a *modest infallibility* of my *adoption*.' Donne preached so often to the dejected, who distrusted their own salvation, out of his knowledge of such a state. He consoles them as he had learned to console himself.

He returns to the fate of our bodies after death in a passage often referred to as an example of his terrible morbidity. He was not deliberately shocking his hearers by describing things of which they had no experience. The most gruesome aspect of a serious outbreak of plague was the accumulation of bodies of those who had collapsed and died in the streets, or who lay dead in houses where all the inhabitants were dying or deadly sick, waiting to be collected in the plague carts and to be trundled together through the streets to rot together in the open plague pits. It might also be said that Donne's horror at the fate of the body after death is the corollary of the conviction that underlies so much of his poetry, and is stated again and again in his sermons, that the body is not the prison of the soul to be sloughed off, but is the means without which 'it could nothing do'. And the whole long first part leads to the affirmation that even from this 'to naturall *reason*, the most *irrecoverable death* of all' God 'shall in a blessed and glorious *resurrection* give mee such an *issue from* this *death*, as shal never passe into any other death, but establish mee into a life that shall last as long as the *Lord of life* himselfe.' Once more he reverts to the first person singular.

The second part of the sermon is briefer, and Donne reminds us of the point he had told us he would make: 'That is *belongs* to *God* and *not* to *man to passe a judgement* upon us at our death.' At the opening of what is perhaps his most famous poem Donne had employed the image of the peaceful death of 'virtuous men'. In July 1627 he had preached the funeral sermon for his friend Magdalen Herbert and spoken of her peaceful Christian death. Six months later, in his Lent sermon, he painted two tradi- tional, contrasting pictures of the dying man: 'he that dies in the Bath of a peaceable, and he that dies upon the wrack of a distracted conscience'. But now, with his own death so near upon him, he remembers that however much a peace- ful death in bed may be prayed for by a Christian, men meet death in many ways, perhaps by sudden accident, or in war, or with their senses and minds disordered by sickness, or in such extremity of bodily pain, or delirium of fever, that they cry out against the God whom they had trusted and had tried to serve. Donne's strength as a preacher, as it is one of his greatest strengths as a poet, is that he constantly recurs, or brings us back, to the 'real state of sublunary nature' and to the 'actual course of the world'. As he preaches he speaks to men from the situation he and they are in. It is no test, he declares, of a man's acceptance that he dies like a lamb, nor of his rejection that he dies raving and cursing in delirium. Judgement is with God alone. He speaks here to those who suffer from his own 'sin of feare' that when they have spun their last thread they will 'perish on the shore'; even more, perhaps, to those haunted by fears for those they had loved and seen die without the marks of a holy death. One of the worst horrors of a visitation of the plague was the constant shrieking and wailing of the dying, the bereaved, and of those driven lunatic.

And so he comes to his last part: a long and detailed meditation on the Passion, beginning with the washing of the disciples' feet and ending with the image of the dying Christ upon the Cross. 'The cross of Christ is dimly seen in Taylor's works. Compare him in this respect with Donne, and you will feel the difference in a moment.'[27] Evelyn Simpson quoted with approval this observation by Coleridge in her early study of Donne's prose; when she came to the last volume of her edition of the sermons and wrote of *Deaths Duell*, she commented:

This is the fullest meditation on our Lord's death which Donne has left us, for if he preached any Good Friday sermons at St. Paul's or St. Dunstan's, he has left us no record of them. This is characteristic of him, for he has told us that to him the Passion of Christ was a subject for adoring love and ecstasy, not for an exercise of rhetorical skill. But now at last, when he knew himself to be a dying man, and the plaudits of men meant nothing to him, he could speak more freely than ever before of the central fact of his religion, of the amazing, unending paradox that God could die, and would die for the love of man.[28]

This long meditation on the Passion is the climax of Donne's preparation for death. I suppose many of us have been struck when looking at some vivid, often terrible, painting of the Crucifixion—I have in mind, particularly, the *Rétable d'Issenheim* by Grünewald, now in the museum at Colmar—by the fact that it was painted for a hospice, to hang before the eyes of the dying in the *salle des agonisants*; and, then, may have remembered a wise retort by C. S. Lewis to some glib comparison between our society and earlier ages: 'Think of a world without anaesthetics.' Or some may have remembered Paul Gerhardt's hymn 'O Haupt voll Blut und Wunden', finely translated by Bridges:

> My days are few, O fail not,
>   With thine immortal power,
> To hold me that I quail not

> In death's most fearful hour:
> That I may fight befriended,
> And see in my last strife
> To me thine arms extended
> Upon the Cross of life.

But, as he makes his own meditation, Donne remembers his congregation. For them, who have time left in this world, he turns his meditation to its classic use, as a means of stimulating the affections to arouse the conscience and direct the will to amendment of life.

Professor Fish at the close of his discussion reminds us of the occasion, adding 'For once, Donne's theatricalism served him well' as he preached, 'gaunt, enfeebled, and dying'. None of Donne's contemporaries described his manner in the pulpit as 'theatrical'. Walton's famous description of Donne preaching is echoed in the elegies printed as tributes in the first edition of his poems in 1633. 'Humility', 'gravity', 'mildness', 'holy fear'—these are some of the terms used to describe Donne preaching. He is contrasted with the 'Sons of Zeal', who

> to reforme
> Their hearers, fiercely at the Pulpit storme,
> And beate the cushion into worse estate,
> Than if they did conclude it reprobate,
> Who can pray out the glasse, then lay about
> Till all Predestination be runne out.

Another elegist tells us that 'the doctrine men', who 'humm'd against him',

> Call'd him a strong-lin'd man, a Macaroon,
> And no way fit to speake to clouted shoone,
> As fine words truly as you would desire,
> But verily, but a bad edifier.

Donne himself in *Deaths Duell* says '*Discourses* of *Religion* should not be *out* of *curiosity* but to *edification*.' We are faced with two conceptions of edification. To Donne the instruction of a congregation in the finer points of the doctrines of Predestination, Election, and Reprobation was 'curiosity'. He thought it his duty to strengthen and confirm the faith of his hearers in those fundamental beliefs that all Christians hold in common, by appealing to theirs hearts and consciences. As another of his elegists wrote:

> Passions excesse for thee wee need not feare,
> Since first by thee our passions hallowed were;
> Thou mad'st our sorrowes, which before had bin
> Onely for the Successe, sorrowes for sinne. . . .
> Nor didst thou only consecrate our teares,
> Give a religious tincture to our feares. . . .
> Pious dissector: thy one houre did treate
> The thousand mazes of the heart's deceipt. . . .

This is by Sidney Godolphin, Suckling's 'Little Sid'. His poem was added in the second edition to the collection of elegies that already contained poems by Lucius Cary (Lord Falkland), Edward Hyde (later Lord Clarendon), and Jasper Mayne, as well as the most famous of the tributes, that by Hyde's close friend Thomas Carew. Donne's admiration for Hooker is well known. Hooker got into trouble for daring to say that not merely a Cardinal but even a Pope might be saved. The fact that Falkland and four of his circle at Great Tew paid homage as young men to Donne is less often noted. Donne stands in a line that runs from Hooker through Great Tew. He believed that in all Christian professions there was a way to salvation, insisted that Christ came to save all men and not only an elect people, that since Scripture spoke of a multitude of the redeemed 'which no man could number', we 'may believe that many more will be saved than lost'. He preached constantly against exclusiveness: against the Roman claim to be the only true Church on the one hand, and, on the other, against 'over-pure despisers of others' and men that 'thinke that no sin can hurt them, because they are *elect*, and that every sin makes every other man a reprobate'. He deplored the additions he saw the Roman Church as having made to the Apostolic Faith, and the divisions among Protestants, caused by what he saw as disagreements over matters beyond our knowledge and impossible to test by experience. Donne had a restless, sceptical, and enquiring mind; but he was neither a philosopher nor a theologian. He was very widely read in the Fathers and in current theological disputations; but his use of the terms of theology and of theological argument in his poetry, and even in his sermons, is illustrative, often ironic, speculative, and ambiguous. In his poem 'The Will', he bequeathed his 'doubtful-nesse' to Schoolmen in the verse in which he gave back to the givers what they had given him. As a layman he had used his wide learning in two great issues that were of momentous difficulty to individual consciences. In *Pseudo-Martyr* he had attempted to persuade Catholics that it was possible to disentangle their spiritual and political loyalties: that Catholics could take the Oath of Allegiance without prejudice to their obedience in spiritual matters to Rome. In *Biathanatos*, which he never published, Donne examined the profoundest of moral problems: whether suicide is in all cases sin. It is the earliest English treatment of the subject and one of the earliest in Europe. He wrote it, he said, 'that to some learned and subtle men which have travelled in this point, some charitable and compassionate men might be added'. His treatment of this dark area of speculation may be fruitfully compared with Burton's in *The Anatomy of Melancholy*, another writer in whose work we can see behind the learning of the text the countenance of one that had 'an aspect as if he pitied men'.

What Donne brought to his late-adopted profession was a fundamental faith that had been tested and proved in need, his experience of life and knowledge of the human heart, and above all his gifts as a poet: his imagination, and his mastery of the rhythms and cadences of speech. Read in their chronological order, his sermons show how more and more he came to feel confidence in his power to bring home to his hearers, by 'heavenly Eloquence', the message with which he felt himself entrusted, employing rhetoric, which can make 'absent and remote things present' to the understanding.[29] I would not claim for *Deaths Duell* that it is one of the greatest of Donne's sermons. It has authority from the circumstances of its composition and delivery, since

> the tongues of dying men
> Enforce attention like deep harmony.

It has also its own power as bringing together many of the concerns that had occupied Donne's heart and mind and conscience since as a young man, nearly forty years before, he had written his Satire 'On Religion', with its final admonition: 'Keepe the truth which thou hast found', and its closing words: 'God himselfe to trust'.

I would not presume to say what *Deaths Duell* will 'actually do' to anyone who will either look at it again, or read it for the first time as a result of this discussion. Who can legislate for the response of others? I do not accept this excited rhetoric about what texts 'actually do', which is replacing the older, soberer emphasis on what they say. I regard the methodology of 'stop and go' as a parody of genuine scientific investigation of the workings of the human brain, providing a spurious justification for what the critic himself arbitrarily chooses to 'do' to, and with, the text. A better way, to my mind, of slowing down the reading process and awakening attention to the nuances of language in the hands of great masters is to read aloud, to oneself, to one's friends, or in a group, or to listen to a good reader. With a sermon particularly it is surely to the point to remember it was heard, not in exactly the same form as we read it in, before it was ever read. It was intended to be taken in by the ear as a continuous discourse.

In 1972 the city of London celebrated the four-hundredth anniversary of the birth of John Donne, a poet who was born and died in the city of London and spent most of his working life there.[30] The week of celebration was a joint enterprise between the Metropolitan Cathedral of St. Paul's and the Mermaid Theatre in Blackfriars. At a commemorative evensong, Paul Schofield read short passages from Donne's sermons before the psalms and lessons. These had been chosen from Psalms and passages of Scripture upon which Donne had preached. For the sermon he read a much abbreviated version of the Christmas sermon that Donne had preached in old St. Paul's in 1624. During two lunch-hours during the week—we were very lucky in the weather—Bernard Miles, standing on the steps outside the north door of St. Paul's, a few yards from where Paul's Cross once stood, to an audience sitting on the stones of the piazza with their sandwiches, and of city workers passing by on their way to lunch, who stopped to see what was going on, and who mostly, having stopped, stayed until the end, read, with the briefest introductions, passages from Donne's sermons. In the hush of the Cathedral at evensong, and in the October sunshine in the lunch-hour outside, hearing the distant hum of the traffic and sitting among this oddly assorted crowd, swollen by passers-by, it was plain to me that John Donne, although dead for over three hundred years, still spoke. The listeners seemed to have no difficulty in following, nor did the reader find any difficulty in reading. Although the listeners listened seriously, they gave no appearance of being harassed or humiliated. On the contrary, many faces showed a serious enjoyment. The experience of reading Professor Fish on Donne's last sermon left me with nothing to take away but an attempt to establish a non-existent category; unless we are to take it that any and every work that assumes that there are matters beyond the reach of human reason is self-consuming. If so, the Bible is the most self-consuming artifact of all.

NOTES

1   *The Philosophy of Literary Form* (2nd edition, New York, 1967), 23.
2   *John Skelton's Poetry* (New Haven and London, 1965), 27–30.
3   *Surprised by Sin* (Berkeley and Los Angeles, 1967), 4.
4   *John Skelton's Poetry*, 258.
5   *Surprised by Sin*, 166–8.
6   *The Use of Poetry and the Use of Criticism*, 131–5. Commenting upon Richards's 'technique or ritual for heightening sincerity', provided in *Practical Criticism* (1929), 290, Eliot ended by observing 'in passing, the intense religious seriousness of Richards's attitude to poetry'.
7   *Surprised by Sin*, 23. No reason is given for supposing that Milton 'relied' on these three 'truths'. It seems more probable that he relied on his readers' familiarity with the suspensions of periodic sentences. All educated people of his age—and *Paradise Lost* was not written for popular consumption—had spent most of their time at school translating such sentences from Latin and composing Latin sentences on their model.

8 *Self-Consuming Artifacts* (Berkeley and California, 1972), 389. The words quoted occur in 'Literature in the Reader: Affective Stylistics', *New Literary History*, ii (Autumn, 1970) reprinted as an Appendix to *Self-Consuming Artifacts*. The *New York Times* (Science Section), 11 March 1980 contained an interesting article on scientific eavesdropping on some of the highest mental activities of the human brain by 'filtering out' electrical 'noise' and isolating voltage changes relating to specific thoughts. A sentence is read at the rate of one word per second. If the sentence makes sense, there is no disturbance in the waves recorded on a screen from electrodes fastened to the subject's brain. But if, instead of being presented with 'It was his first day at work', the brain is presented with the sentence 'He spread his warm bread with socks', in a quarter of a second a 'wave spike appears on the screen'. This can be regarded as a scientific investigation, although it does not seem to take us very far towards explaining how we read *Paradise Lost*.

9 *Self-Consuming Artifacts*, 1–3.

10 Ibid., 380.

11 *Sermons*, ii. 282. All quotations from Donne's sermons are from the edition, in ten volumes, edited by George R. Potter and Evelyn M. Simpson (Berkeley and Los Angeles, 1953–62).

12 *Self-Consuming Artifacts*, 156–7.

13 F. E. Hutchinson (*Works of George Herbert* (Oxford, 1941), 535) quotes H. C. Beeching's admirable note in *Lyra Sacra*: '*Is*, i.e. is in itself, or unchangeably; it is what it is by God's immediate ordinance.'

14 The Psalmist, throughout the entire long psalm, continually refers to 'thy word', 'thy commandment', 'thy testimonies' as stable in a world of change. 'I know that all things pass away, but thy commandment is exceeding broad.' Ps. 119:96.

15 *Sermons*, ii. 74.

16 The title 'Deaths Duell' had been used as the title of a book entered in the Stationers' Register three months earlier, Walter Coleman's *La Danse Machabre or Deaths Duell*. It was published after Donne's sermon as Coleman added after his poems some doggerel verses objecting to the printer's theft of his title. See Geoffrey Keynes, *TLS*, 24 September 1938.

17 *Sermons*, vii. 133–4.

18 *Sermons*, ii. 170–1.

19 *Sermons*, vi. 18.

20 *Sermons*, iii. 359.

21 *Sermons*, viii. 225

22 *Self-Consuming Artifacts*, 44, 61, 69 and 60.

23 Ibid., 45.

25 *Sermons* viii. 174.

25 See F. P. Wilson, *The Plague in Shakespeare's London* (Oxford, 1927), chapter V, for an account of the Great Plague and of the panic in 1630 when it was feared that another 'great plague' was on the way.

26 Preaching on the text 'Remember now thy Creator', in his Valediction Sermon of 1619, Donne strenuously argued that 'memory can

go no farther then the creation; and therefore we have no means to conceive or apprehend any thing of God before that. When men therefore speak of decrees of reprobation, decrees of condemnation, before decrees of creation; this is beyond the counsail of the holy Ghost here, *Memento creatoris*, Remember the Creator, for this is to remember God a condemner before he was a creator.' *Sermons*, ii. 245–6.

27   Coleridge, *Table Talk* (1835), i. 168.

28   *Sermons*, x. 35. Evelyn Simpson in a footnote gives a passage from an early sermon: 'But for that I shall be short, and rather leave you . . . to meditate of the sufferings of Christ, when you are gone, then pretend to expresse them here. The *passion* of Christ Jesus is rather an amazement, an astonishment, an extasie, a consternation, then an instruction.' *Sermons*, ii. 132.

29   'How barren a thing is Arithmetique? (and yet Arithmetique will tell you, how many single graines of sand, will fill this hollow Vault to the Firmament) How empty a thing is Rhetorique? (and yet Rhetorique will make absent and remote things present to your understanding) How weake a thing is Poetry? (and yet Poetry is a counterfeit Creation, and makes things that are not, as though they were) How infirme, how impotent are all assistances, if they be put to express this Eternity?' *Sermons*, iv. 87.

30   See Barbara Everett's Chatterton Lecture to the British Academy in 1972 for an admirable discussion of 'Donne: A London Poet'. (*Proceedings of the British Academy*, lxviii, 1972 (1974)).

Chapter V

Narratives and Fictions

Around the middle of this century, after the end of the war, there was a very marked shift of critical attention and critical theory away from poetry and towards the novel. Thus, F. R. Leavis, who had been concerned in *New Bearings in English Poetry* in 1932 with redrawing the old map of English poetry on the lines suggested by Eliot in his early essays, and with tracing 'the line of wit', turned his attention to the novel and in 1948 redrew the old map of the history of the novel in *The Great Tradition*. Eliot and Richards had shown little interest in the novel or in criticism of the novel, and the same was true of the founders of the New Criticism in America, John Crowe Ransom and Cleanth Brooks. Their theories about the nature of poetry were derived from a belief that the quintessence of poetry was to be found in the lyric. They, therefore, took little interest in poetical narrative and even less in prose fiction. A sign of a shift of interest was the new turn given to the old critical quarrels over *Paradise Lost* by the appearance in 1947 of A. J. A. Waldock's *Paradise Lost and Its Critics*. Waldock, frankly recognizing that the novel was the dominant literary genre of his century, approached Milton's epic with the expectations and standards created in any 'modern reader' by his reading in novels, and found it by these standards seriously wanting. Throughout the fifties and sixties the shift of emphasis from a criticism based on concepts of the nature of poetry and of poetic language to a criticism concerned with narrative fictions can be seen. It derived much of its theoretical basis from the theory and practice of Henry James. To revert again for a moment to *Paradise Lost*, the arguments over Milton's style gave place to arguments over his conduct of the narrative; and in Joseph Summers's *The Muse's Method* in 1962, the concept of the 'guilty reader' was borrowed from Jamesian criticism to become, allied to his theory of the reading process, the basis of Stanley Fish's *Surprised by Sin*.

The older interest in the nature of poetic language and the new interest in narrative have in common a high degree of abstraction from actuality. They share a concern with a kind of Platonic idea, a general and universal concept of a poem or a narrative, which overrides interest in the rich variety of poems and narratives that have appeared through the ages, under the constraints of our temporal existence as historical beings, living under the pressures of our individual temperaments and individual experiences, our cultural inheritance, and the society of which we are members. The methods of literary criticism that were developed out of the concern with the nature of poetry and of poetic language—the discoveries of manifold ambiguities, ironies, double and triple meanings, complexities, and patterns of imagery—were developed with a high degree of virtuosity, ingenuity, and zest. Explications, interpretations, new readings proliferated, the texts serving as a kind of *champ de bataille*, arena, or lists, on which champions displayed their originality and ingenuity. The same thing has now happened with the new interest in narrative in general, in which distinctions between different kinds of narrative are disregarded in favour of the discovery of occult resemblances between things apparently unlike. A most striking example of this is the brilliant and lively series of lectures given by Frank Kermode during his term as Charles Eliot Norton Professor of Poetry, published in 1979 as *The Genesis of Secrecy*, and subtitled 'on the interpretation of narrative'. Nobody who reads this book can help being struck by the intellectual energy and enthusiasm with which Kermode has entered the field of Biblical criticism, the massive reading he has done in a subject of formidable complexity, and the striking incidental comments he makes out of his wide range of reading in modern novels and in modern literary theory on problems of interpretation in the Gospel of Mark. The lectures, as published, are written with their author's customary wit and elegance, and buttressed by a most formidable array of notes.

When I met Kermode in London, on his return from Harvard but before his lectures were published, he told me that they were to be concerned with the criticism of the New Testament, and that he found the subject of absorbing interest and intended to pursue it further. It was impossible not to be impressed by, and not to feel sympathy with, his obvious pleasure in having entered upon a new and rich field of study, and I greatly looked forward to reading the lectures when they appeared. I had a personal reason for being interested, as many years before I had ventured as a literary critic to discuss an attempt by a New Testament scholar, the late Dr Austin Farrer, to apply the methods of modern literary criticism to the Gospel of Mark.[1] In a lecture to the British Academy on 'Spenser and the Allegorists' in 1962, Kermode had twice, in discussing archetypal criticism, referred with approval to my lectures, and, in 1966, in *The Sense of an Ending*, I appeared once more as having 'justly', in his view, attacked modern theologians and literary critics 'for their typological obsessions' as diminishing 'the force and actuality of the Gospels, as they do of secular litera-ture'.[2] He returned to the topic in 1969 in an article on 'The Structures of Fiction',[3] in which, owning that 'we are in and will for some time remain in a period of which the preferred instruments for the description of novels and their truth are those of structural analysis', he confessed 'to a strong feeling that novels are extremely resistant to these instruments, whatever may be said of other kinds of fiction'. To illustrate this he took 'three fictions, which are not novels, in which three different ways of determining structure and meaning' can be employed: a Chinook story, analysed by an anthropologist, who assumes that the characteristics of such a story will be in accordance with the culture in which it has arisen; the myth of Oedipus, analysed by Lévi-Strauss, which discovers a universal occult structure, represented by an algebraic formula (as a is to b, so is x to y); and the Passion narrative of St. Mark, as analysed by Austin Farrer, which discovers the narrative to be structured typologically. He then examined a novel, Conrad's *Under Western Eyes*, to distinguish novels from folk-tales, myths, or gospels, as having structures 'that are plural, inaccessible without severe instrumental interference, and possessing no validity or interest except in union with acts of idomatic interpretation'. It might be objected that the novel chosen was a particularly complex one; but I imagine that most readers of novels who read the article would have been grateful for its firm rejection of the idea that novels can be reduced to some 'central determined structure we can isolate as fundamental'.

I realized, on reading his lectures on *The Classic*,[4] that Kermode had moved beyond his rejection of structural analysis as an adequate instrument for dealing with the plurality of novels to a position that appeared to deny the possibility of reading a text with the cultural presuppositions of the writer in mind, and regarded the possibilities of interpretation as infinite. Even so, when I read *The Genesis of Secrecy*, which is devoted to the interpretation of the Gospel of Mark, I was, I confess, dismayed at the combination of great intellectual activity, and great enjoyment in the exercise of interpretative ingenuities, with the melancholy negativism of the conclusion: the sense that the whole enterprise was a kind of game played for its own sake, which was ultimately pointless. My objection to the critical methods employed by Dr Farrer was that, while arguing that the Gospel of Mark as we have it was the work of a single author, they made this author into a disembodied imagination. My objection to Kermode's treatment of Mark is of the same kind. It treats the author as a mere exemplar of timeless laws governing the development of narratives of all and every kind. Abandoning the notion that it is possible to arrive by rational argument, if not at absolute and complete truth, at least at some statements that may be considered truer than others, it holds before us as the object of our study the ideal of being 'interesting'. This raises the question 'Who to?'. No doubt it is to others who enjoy playing the same kind of game; but ultimately to the performer himself, alone before the book as he is alone before the book of the world. The pursuit of knowledge and true judgement, which can be communicated and shared by others, is abandoned in the hunt for some occult meaning that remains forever undiscoverable and perhaps does not exist at all.

Kermode's book was to me deeply disappointing, and to use his own word 'unfollowable'. In spite of his suggestion that we cannot, or should not, distinguish fictitious from historical narratives, he makes large historical generalizations, but is extremely chary of providing us with any dates. This is particularly troubling in his treatment of the allegorizing of Scripture, which is spoken of as if it were unknown before the Christian era, and in an extraordinary passage, which he himself describes as 'skipping across millennia of interpretation', we zoom from the joining of the Old Testament to the New, placed late in the second century, to an early fifteenth-century theologian, Jean Gerson, and, after a parenthetical reference to 'one of the main causes of the Reformation', we go back to the twelfth-century Joachim da Fiore, and the imperial propaganda of the Emperor Frederick II, and end up in the Third Reich of Hitler. This dizzying ride to and fro through the centuries rests upon the notion that the literal sense, which Kermode, like Stanley Fish, prefers to call the 'carnal' sense, was superseded by the spiritual sense, which became the 'true sense'.[5] The same notion recurs later in a discussion of the parable of the Good Samaritan, where, though it is said that 'there had long been a literalist opposition to free allegory', Luther's rejection of it was, we are told, decisive.[6] This is history on the model of *1066 and All That*. It reminds me of a cartoon in *Punch* during the war where a feudal baron was shown instructing his retainers that the Middle Ages would stop 'to-morrow at 11-0 ack emma'. Kermode ignores the insistence of all important commentators from Augustine onwards that there is a 'main sense', or 'principal intention', or 'literal sense', which may, as Aquinas and others make clear, be itself figuratively expressed by metaphor or other tropes, and that it is on the basis of acceptance of this normative sense that moral, mystical, or anagogical senses may be found and may become traditional for purposes of edification. The same process can be seen operating in any good sermon in any period. Indeed, without this finding of something to draw out of a text it is difficult to see how any sermons could ever be preached. The type of application made to the moral and spiritual needs of a congregation may vary very widely. In the nineteenth century there was most commonly an emphasis on the moral implications; today frequently it is on the social and political; but it rests on acceptance of a primary sense which, as Kermode rightly notes, does not greatly vary. Augustine is not only famous for the kind of interpretations that Kermode quotes; he was also the author of a long commentary in twelve books on the literal sense of Genesis, *De Genesi ad litteram*. It is a sign of his decisive break with Manichaean and Neo-Platonic conceptions, of his acceptance of the Judeo-Christian belief in the creation of the world by the word or *Fiat* of the one and only God. Kermode's generalizations ignore what historical scholarship has taught us about the study of the Bible in the Middle Ages,[7] and what he would have found if he had ever had to make use of the standard guide to the interpretation of Scripture in the later Middle Ages, the Paris Vulgate *cum Glossa Ordinaria*, with citations from the Fathers in its margins.

I find a similar confusion in his discussion of the notion of 'fulfilment', where a distinction that is clearly made in a sentence from Justin Martyr, which he quotes, is overlooked, and we are told that reference to types and testimonies 'in its extreme form . . . implies the abolition of the Old Testament except in its role as a type source for the New—in short "the total destruction of its historical character" '.[8] Types and testimonies are not the same thing and should not be treated as interchangeable terms. The whole conception of *figura*, as discussed in Auerbach's famous book *Mimesis*, rested on the acceptance of both the type and its fulfilment as historical. That Moses leading the children of Israel out of bondage in Egypt and across the Red Sea was seen as prefiguring the deliverance of the new Israel from the bondage of sin and death by the death of Christ, did not imply that Moses was not a historical figure, and the deliverance of the children of Israel was not a historical event. 'Sometimes', wrote Justin Martyr, in a passage Kermode quotes from Jean Daniélou, 'the Holy Spirit . . . has caused something to be done which was a type of what was to happen, sometimes he uttered words concerning what was to come about, phrasing them as if they referred to things taking place then or even having already taken place.' *Things done: words uttered.* Things done are the mighty acts of God, deliverances brought about by men, who obeyed a call of the God who had brought the world into being and who intervenes in its history through his chosen vessels: Noah, Abraham, Moses, great fundamental types, in whom are performed the redemptive acts of God in human history. And on the other hand there are words uttered: 'speech above a mortal mouth'. This is Ben Jonson's definition of poetry, and there are many poets who have believed themselves to have been inspired to 'something like prophetic strain'. These are words by men whose lips have been touched by a live coal, who have heard the voice of the Lord crying 'Who shall I send?', and have replied 'Here I am, send me', and have then been commanded 'Go, tell'. Kermode is rightly and naturally interested more in the testimonies, and the use of them to develop and colour narrative by the evangelists, than in the types. I am not reproaching him for this; but for his failure to recognize the fundamental historicism that Christianity derived from Judaism and shares with it: the emphasis on things done as revelatory; and that in both Judaism and Christianity rituals that re-enacted saving acts pre-existed and exercised control over the literary documents that he is concerned with. Hebrew historicism and Hebrew prophecy and poetry are distinct modes. Thus the passages quoted in a note from Irenaeus as testimonies fulfilled in Christ's Passion are all from the prophets and the psalms, the prophetic and poetical, not the historical, books of the Bible. Kermode ignores, as William Empson pointed out in a review, C. H. Dodd's main arguments about the kind of testimonies used, and distorts his views when he says that he had 'a highly developed sense of ways in which a factual narrative could be constructed "according to the Scriptures"',[9] which almost implies that a story could be wholly made up from testimonies alone. I think I could quite easily, if I wished to, construct a narrative of the deaths of Hitler and Eva Braun in the burning bunker in Berlin as being 'according to the Scriptures'. The use of 'proof texts' would greatly colour the details and episodes if I were to do it from memory of what I had read and heard thirty years ago and not with Trevor-Roper's book *The Last Days of Hitler* open before me. It would not be history, but it would not either be pure fiction. The proof texts would be interpretative, but they would be applied to my memory, no doubt faulty, of what, in this case, I had read, and not heard, of what had actually occurred. Some kind of rudimentary narrative of events is required before proof texts are sought to validate it as a fulfilment. Kermode seems so interested in development and interpretation of narrative that he appears not to be concerned with narrative itself, or with its core of events, fictive or not.

Kermode has a very acute sense of his own historical position and situation and makes many statements about what 'we' today must necessarily feel and think. This certainty goes along with an almost total scepticism as to the possibility of scholarship arriving at any coherent conception of the historical situation in which writers of the past found themselves and wrote. There is a continuing assumption that because we cannot know everything, we cannot know anything; that the only alternative to certainty is total ignorance. It is not until more than half way through the book that we have a mention of Christian communities, and even here it is only to suggest that such communities had notebooks containing testimonies, comparable to the collection of 'proof texts about the Messiah found in a cave at Qumram'.[10] A little later it is suggested that the differences between the four canonical gospels 'are no doubt due to the varying needs and interests of the communities for whom the evangelists originally wrote, and to their own diverse theological predispositions',[11] but near the end we are balked again: 'whatever we may find to say about the community for which it [that is, Mark's Gospel] was originally written (and the evidence will come largely from the gospel itself, in defeating circularity) it is far beyond us to reproduce the tacit understandings that existed between this dead writer and his audience.'[12] So we come to the conclusion that 'we have to think of the book as a sample of what we take literature to be' which seems no conclusion at all. We had earlier been warned that we should be moving 'toward what may be a cheerless conclusion', that perhaps 'at the heart of Mark' there is no secret at all; 'but rather some habit of narrative paradox or conjunction that might, in the end, be best represented without the use of words, in a diagram or by algebra'.[13]

But in other parts of the book, some facts and even some dates are, even roughly, suggested as acceptable. Discussing the original abrupt end of Mark's Gospel, with the women fleeing from the empty tomb 'for they were afraid', Kermode finds it hard to see 'why the gospel ... should stop before it had fairly reached that part that seemed most important to Paul; by Mark's time it had been preached for an entire generation'. This is a firm historical statement, implying that there is a consensus that Kermode accepts on the date of Mark's Gospel and of Paul's first letter to the Corinthians. In parenthesis, I think it is a little odd to write as if Mark, although in its original form it contained no narratives of Resurrection appearances, which Paul a generation before had referred to, does not proclaim the Resurrection. The women find the stone rolled back, and the young man seated on the right side, clothed in a long white garment, declares 'He is risen, he is not here, behold the place where they laid him.'[14] Paul, however, makes two later welcome appearances. The same epistle is cited as evidence for the existence of 'early reports of a Last Supper, which by the time of Paul's first letter to the Corinthians had been fixed as part of the liturgical tradition; and Mark's account of the breaking of the bread and drinking of wine is strongly liturgical';[15] and on the next page we are reminded that Paul's account had linked the Last Supper with the betrayal. A more sustained reading of the authentic epistles of Paul might have provided a little insight into the nature of the Christian communities among which the Gospels arose. Even more remarkable, for here we are given precise dates, is the reference to Pilate, who, we are told, 'was, of course, an historical character', Procurator of Judea from AD 26 to 36, and, according to Josephus, a hard man, though, 'as C. K. Barrett observes, "he had successors whose little finger was thicker than his loins"'.[16] The mists clear away for a moment here, but only to descend again in the next chapter, when Barthes is quoted as telling us that 'the fact can only exist linguistically, as a term in a discourse', and a note informs us that 'the sentence "Napoleon died at Saint Helena on May 5, 1821" does not, for the semiologist, constitute something that is historically true, but merely shows that there exist in our culture codes such that sentences of this kind connote "historical truth"'.[17] Kermode owns very frankly more than once that he finds it difficult to keep hold of such ideas and that they require of him 'a special effort' that he is 'unwilling to make'. As I read his book I felt all the time that his natural good sense and his literary sensibility were constantly breaking through his attempt to accept these sterile and stultifying procedures, like the cheerfulness that broke in on Johnson's friend's attempt to become a philosopher. I even wondered at times whether I was being a 'guilty reader' in attempting to take the discussion seriously: whether the whole performance was to be read ironically as an exposure of the futility of the attempt to keep literary criticism pure from any contact with history or common sense.

I must own that I have no competence to enter the field of New Testament scholarship. I lack both Hebrew and Aramaic and have only rudimentary schoolgirl Greek. I am also unfamiliar with recent work on the subject. I became involved by accident some thirty or so years ago when I was invited to a conference between philosophers, theologians and literary critics, called on the initiative of the philosophers, who wanted to discuss more interesting uses of language than those that were then concerning the current school of linguistic philosophers. The subject was 'imagery'. It was a slightly absurd occasion as the discussion was largely concerned with the current German debate on 'Demythologising', and with the work of Dr Bultmann, its most celebrated exponent. His views were the main concern of the New Testament scholars present, and his name constantly recurred, but none of the philosophers had heard of him, and I was the only literary critic who had some idea, a little hazy, of his position. This put me in the awkward position of having to sum up the rather inconsequent discussion and write a short report. To a lesser degree another scholar, also not present, hovered over the meeting.

This was Austin Farrer, then chaplain of Trinity College, Oxford, whose Bampton lectures, *The Glass of Vision*, had made a great impression. Farrer bulks large in Kermode's lectures, although he, while very courteously and kindly correcting some of my ignorant arguments against him, generously conceded there was some justice in my complaint generally.[18] Bultmann does not occur in Kermode's lectures, whereas twenty-five or thirty years ago he would have been at the centre of any discussion. I do not say this to reproach Kermode for neglecting him; but to suggest that not to be up-to-date does not necessarily disqualify me from questioning some of the fundamental assumptions on which Kermode's lectures rest. Bultmann seemed very important in the years just after the war. He seems less important now. Existentialism is no longer very fashionable. On the other hand there are some older works that constitute landmarks, and which anyone discussing a subject of study cannot disregard. I have in mind here that Kermode makes only one reference to what in English is called 'form-criticism', and that is to dismiss it airily as 'an institutional prejudice' used to 'disarm exegesis founded on more interesting personal prejudices'. Even more extraordinary is the fact that it is not until the final summing-up that we find a reference to a 'quantity of oral material' and 'perhaps a few pieces of paper' as providing the writer of the Gospel of Mark with the content of his narrative.

Let me begin by accepting that all narrative interprets events, whether the events have actually occurred or are fictions. Even someone giving a bare account of 'what happened' selects by a criterion of significance and consequence. Let me also accept that all narrative is imaginative in that it presents images of actions and behaviour. But granting that, does it make sense to refer to the evangelists as 'imaginative writers' in the same sense as we refer to Henry James or James Joyce or Henry Green as imaginative writers? Can we call whoever wrote down Mark's Gospel (accepting as possible the hypothesis that the text as we have it is the work of a single writer) an *author*, that is an originator, in the same sense as we can call a modern novelist an *author*? The origin of *What Maisie Knew* was a simple hint of a possible subject, a tiny *donnée*; but it was enough to set James's imagination working, creating episodes and scenes, developing characters to surround the small figure of Maisie, who has to make her way somehow in a treacherous and unreliable world. James writes under no necessity towards his readers except to interest and please them, and convince them of the probability, the imaginative truth, of the tale he tells and of the behaviour of the actors in it. More importantly for him, he is guided by his own conscience as an artist to develop to his own satisfaction all the potentialities that he discovers in the simple initial situation he began from. There are no other restraints upon him. The responsibility for what he writes is wholly his own. The writer of the Gospel of Mark was 'making up' his narrative in quite a different sense and was writing under severe restraints. He was compiling, or putting together, material which had come down by word of mouth, for some use, possibly liturgical, in the very communities in which it had been preserved and repeated. Kermode, more than once, in spite of the admiration he expresses in his preface for the 'scholarly rigour and discipline of the best Biblical study', as 'high enough to be, in many ways, exemplary to us all' (meaning by 'us all', I suppose, literary scholars), expresses surprise at the 'naïveté' of professional exegetes. I do not know what he takes to be the antonym for '*naïveté*', but I suspect it would be 'sophistication' in its sad modern use as a term of praise. I find it extremely naïve for a literary scholar to show no appreciation of the distinction between a work originating in oral traditions and showing clear marks of memorial preservation, and a work originating in a known and extant literary source, which a writer has handled and reshaped freely, as Shakespeare handled Plutarch or the Chronicles, and, even more, with a work originating in a writer's invention of a story and his free shaping, expansion, and development of it into a work of art. If we are going to insist on a disjunction between speech and writing, *parole et écriture*, we must give up any attempt to study antique texts, based on oral tradition and written to be recited or read aloud. And perhaps, for reading the Gospel of Mark, *naïveté* is not such a bad qualification. In the best sense of the word it is a naïve text that offers itself to the world and not to a specially trained and educated audience. How can we compare, with any hope of arriving at any interpretative or literary judgement, enigmas and puzzles put in by a highly self-conscious literary artist, in a vast, expansive, encyclopaedic work such as *Ulysses*, whose author once said that they were put in 'to keep the professors busy for centuries', with a writer putting together stories, brief sayings, parables, dialogues, as prelude to a continuous narrative of the Passion, matter which had lived and been shaped in the memories and speech of men as it passed by word of mouth, had been embodied in rites celebrated and hymns sung, which is set down with such reserve and concision, at times showing signs of being learnt oral material.[19] It is not set down as a document, containing secret wisdom for a few, for adepts, or initiates, or to use Kermode's word, 'insiders', but for all who have 'ears to hear'. The enigmas and riddles which Kermode finds in Mark lie in the nature of the material he is presenting and handling, not, as with Joyce, in the intentions of an author. He, like Paul, and to use Paul's words, is 'delivering what he also received' to any who will in turn receive it. I wish Kermode had read a much older book than those he cites, written by two scholars for a lay public, *The Riddle of the New Testament* by Edwin Hoskyns and Noel Davey, published in 1930.

'The gospels sound like history, and that they do so is the consequence of an extraordinary rhetorical feat,'[20] writes Kermode. It is a little odd that he cites as an example 'the rhetorical success' of Defoe's *Apparition of Mrs. Veal*, for we know now that the striking realistic detail of Mrs Veal appearing in her scoured silk dress to her friend Mrs Bargrave was not put in by that skilful rhetorician Daniel Defoe 'to lend artistic verisimilitude to an otherwise bald and unconvincing narrative'. It was part of the recorded account of Mrs Bargrave herself, telling the story of how her friend Mrs Veal appeared to her in her scoured silk frock at the very hour in which she died. The rhetorical feat, if it really deserves to be called such, was Mrs

Bargrave's, not Defoe's, who merely, as a good journalist, gave currency to her naïve story. Kermode then briefly examines the story of Sidney's gesture when lying wounded on the battlefield at Zutphen.

I will begin by taking a trivial anecdote to illustrate both what can happen in oral transmission and also my belief that, although no narrative is wholly transparent on historical reality, all narratives are not therefore totally opaque, and that there are ways by which we can test their degree of reliability. In *The Oxford Book of Literary Anecdotes*, published in 1975, James Sutherland included the following anecdote about Oscar Wilde, who died in 1900, owning that he had been told it but was 'unable to supply a written source':

In his *viva voce* examination for 'Divvers'[21] at Oxford, Oscar Wilde was required to translate from the Greek version of the New Testament, which was one of the set books. The passage chosen was from the story of the Passion. Wilde began to translate easily and accurately. The examiners were satisfied, and told him that was enough. Wilde ignored them and continued to translate. After another attempt the examiners succeeded in stopping him, and told him they were satisfied with his translation. 'Oh, do let me go on', said Wilde, 'I want to see how it ends.'

I happened to ask an American friend, Professor Louis Martz, whether he knew the story, and he told me he had heard it when an undergraduate, which would make it current around 1930; but he said that the incident, as he was told it, occurred on Wilde's first night in gaol. He was reading the Gospel of St. Mark, and when the warder came in with his supper Oscar cried out, 'Go away, Go away—I want to see how it ends.'

It seems obvious that this is a version corrupted in oral transmission across the Atlantic, which substitutes for an Oxford examination that obliged Wilde to read the Gospels a situation in which the only book he would have at hand would be the Bible. The words are unchanged, but the point has become different. In the Oxford version, the remark is a piece of impertinence; Wilde is trying to shock his examiners by pretending not to have read the Gospels.

In prison even Wilde would hardly have wanted to shock a warder, and the point becomes that Wilde really *had* managed to escape knowledge of the story of the Passion. This hardly needs disproof by reference to his writings and early religiosity. I then discovered a written source: *Son of Oscar Wilde* by Vyvyan Holland, Wilde's younger son, published in 1954. He had been hurried abroad with his brother, given another name, told nothing of what had happened to his father, and only told he must not mention him or tell anyone his real name. It was not until he was grown up that he learned about his father and met in England friends still loyal to his father's memory, from whom he learned about him. He gives no authority for his story, but although not published until 1954 he probably heard it around 1920.

My father's knowledge of Greek was profound; but it was due more to a prodigious memory than to hard work. Such was his love of the language that he remembered every word he ever read in it, and acquired, in consequence, a vast Greek vocabulary. A story is told of a *viva voce* examination in Greek. My father, being confident that he could pass any *vive voce* examination in Greek without any preparation, had not even troubled to look at it; and the examiner, suspecting this and being anxious to teach my father a lesson, told him to turn to Chapter 27 of the Acts of the Apostles and to start translating. This chapter is probably the most difficult in the whole of the New Testament, being the description of St. Paul's shipwreck on his way to Italy; it contains a number of obscure nautical terms which no one could be expected to know unless they had studied them. My father translated it perfectly, and when the foiled examiner told him that he had done enough, he replied, 'Please may I go on? I want to see what happened to St. Paul.'[22]

This is surely the original story. It is much tamer than the other versions, as nothing of any importance hangs on knowledge of how St. Paul managed to get safely to shore. The story is told to illustrate Wilde's knowledge of Greek and his retort is not to shock his examiners but to make clear he has not prepared a translation but is translating at sight. It remains an impertinence, but not of the same kind. The story would seem to go back to his Oxford days and his reputation among his contemporaries. Although other candidates waiting their turn would have been present, and vivas were open to the public, there is no suggestion that this was reported by someone who had actually heard it. It is only 'a story'. It is just possible that the story originated in some boast of Wilde's as to how he floored his examiners. Even so, it is inherently improbable, as the request to be allowed to go on would, if I know anything of Oxford examiners, have invited the stuffy retort: 'You may satisfy your curiosity, Mr Wilde, later and elsewhere.' If a biographer referred to it at all it would be only as evidence of Wilde's reputation as an undergraduate.

You may wonder why I have spent time on this frivolous little story. I did so because it patently *is* frivolous. Nothing of the slightest importance hangs on it. It circulated because it was amusing, and became more so, and in a different way, as it lived on. There was no responsibility on anyone telling it to try to 'get it right'. The story of Sidney on the battlefield at Zutphen giving up his drink of water to a wounded soldier with the words 'Thy necessity is greater than mine', resembles the Wilde story in that Fulke Greville wrote it down some twenty-five years after it happened, if it did happen. He gives no source; but that does not prove that he had no source. Is it not at least probable that Greville who described himself on his tomb as 'friend of Sir Philip Sidney', when he heard with a dismay felt all over England, and even in Europe, that Sidney was dead, would have tried to discover from those near him when he fell, as well as from those who watched his lingering death, the circumstances of Sidney's end? Kermode points out that Greville approved of characters in books being exemplary and that he 'presented Sidney as a model of virtue'. This is true; but the fact that like Sidney he believed art should be exemplary, does not mean that he thought of himself as a romancer writing to improve, and, while he does present Sidney as wholly admirable, does it follow that he would have felt a desire to 'paint the lily' or gild the 'refined gold' of Sidney's life by making up a story? Kermode adds that it has been pointed out that 'Greville seems to have been remembering a passage in Plutarch's *Life of Alexander*'. But

Sidney would have known his Plutarch too and he might well have been inspired to his action by the memory of a magnanimous action by an ancient hero, as well as by the Gospel reference to a 'cup of cold water'. Kermode concludes: 'Whether it happened or not, the offer of the drink is what ideally ought to have happened.'[23] The implication seems to be that because it is 'what ideally ought to have happened', it most probably did not. I think myself the odds are a little more evenly balanced.

Let me take one more anecdote:[24] Lockhart's report that just before he died Scott sent for him and said to him, nobody else being present, 'be a good man—be virtuous—be religious—be a good man—nothing else will give you any comfort when you come to lie here'. Here we have a direct first-hand report from Scott's son-in-law, writing his father-in-law's life. Grierson, in his life of Scott, rejected this as a 'pious myth—a concession to the censorious piety of the Evangelical age'. He noted the evidence of Scott's daughter, Sophia, that 'for the last fortnight his life was a miracle, life was only kept going by opiates; his mind never returned for an instant'; that before this Scott was irritable and restless and incoherent, and that his old friend Laidlaw found him in a senseless stupor. Finally Grierson cites a letter to Lockhart from a 'lady relative of Scott', who wrote: 'When you write anything of the last melancholy weeks at Abbotsford I think it will be most valuable to mention any of the few remarks he uttered when his mind was clear of a religious tendency, such as I heard he said occasionally "Oh be virtuous! It is one's only comfort in a dying state".' On the other hand, one could point to the stoicism with which Scott through life endured pain, the evident piety of the *Journal*, the fact that, although Scott disliked the 'unco guid' and fanatics, he was throughout life a believer, and the whole, unforced, strong moral feeling of his novels. If his mind *had* cleared for a short while and he *had* been able to speak articulately, it is the kind of thing he might well have said. A biographer has to make a decision here and there is a strong element of uncertainty. But if Grierson was right to reject the story, we still have to ask *why* Lockhart invented an episode with himself as the only witness. Did he do so to cover up a too painful truth; but then why need he say anything? Why not just let Scott drift into death unconscious? Did he invent the episode because he felt assured that this or something like this Scott would have said, if his mind had cleared, and he was concerned to end his story by something in accordance with what he felt to be a general truth about Scott's attitude to life? Or again are we to look upon the 'lady relative' as being the inventor of the story; or, when she writes that she had heard Scott said occasionally something of the sort, had she really been told it and who by? Has Lockhart only moved to the end something Scott had said earlier? This is an interpretative problem; but it is surely a quite different kind of problem, and we would bring quite different criteria to bear if we were discussing the truth of the words Dickens puts into the mouth of little Paul Dombey dying, or of poor Jo of Tom-All-Alone's. There is no external evidence we can bring to bear here, except our general experience of life, and if we think Dickens here was falsifying the truth, the standard of truth he was working to is not the same as the truth which Lockhart knows his readers expect from him and by which we must assume he was assessing his own writing.

It seems only too likely that we shall reach no conclusions except diagrammatic or algebraical ones, if we insist on disregarding the different motives for which people tell stories, and their circumstances. We may begin with a person in the witness box, who takes an oath, or else affirms, that he will 'tell the truth, the whole truth, and nothing but the truth'. The believer, who is willing to take the oath on the Testament, held up before the court in his right hand, is at least allowed a merciful escape clause in making this unfulfillable declaration of intent—'So help me God!' He is led through his prepared story by learned counsel, and then faced with cross-examination by an equally learned counsel, when gaps in his memory and contrary evidence by other witnesses are exposed to cast doubt upon his testimony. It is for the members of the jury to interpret and judge between the various stories they listen to and assess the summing up. Nobody would be prepared to say the system never results in a miscarriage of justice; but I do not think in an imperfect world that a better system has been found. Then there is a person at a dinner-table, relating with a good deal of deliberate heightening and colouring of the imagination—making, as we say, a good tale out of it— something that had happened the other day. He would be justly irritated if somebody present interrupted the flow of his narrative by pedantic corrections of points of detail in what was not being given as testimony, but was told to entertain and amuse. Do we bring the same standards of interpretation and criticism to bear on a biography, whose author is under an obligation to weigh different kinds of evidence, judge the reliability of witnesses, as well as of written documents, establish a chronology by records and inferences, weigh statements by his subject against what was said by others, and not suppress uncomfortable facts, as we bring to a judgement of an autobiography or a personal memoir? The writer of one is aiming at as large a measure of objectivity as is possible, and can be criticized for omissions and suppressions and misunderstandings of the documents; the other is free to choose what the writer thinks has been most important in his life, or to treat one aspect only of his experience, to speak of other people simply as he met them and as they impressed him. We expect, and allow for, and enjoy a strongly subjective and imaginative colouring here. Or if we turn to fictions, can we fruitfully compare a traditional ballad, taken down from a singer who has learned it, and is singing it to a tune he has also learned, in verse with traditional refrains and formulaic phrases—who may modify what he has learnt, perhaps deliberately, or by unconscious memorial changes, but can only do so within defined limits—with the work of a novelist? And here again we have to ask, what kind of novelist?

Kermode began his lectures with a brilliant, amusing, elegant and entertaining game with a novel by Henry Green, *Party Going*, his justification for his performance being that the orthodox view of the 'literary establishment' is that nothing in a narrative is random and meaningless, and that if it appears so to the untutored reader, it is a challenge to the professional to solve the riddle and discover a significance that will make all the details of a narrative cohere. I do not think he really believes in his own performance here, and think such tenacious worrying of the text of this highly suggestive and 'foggy' novel wrongs it, and disregards its curious air of vagueness and accident and its haunting sense that the 'party is over'. Kermode disarmingly owns this in his excellent paragraph on another of Green's novels, *Loving*, and in his remarks on Green's stylistic eccentricities and his 'beautiful wilfulness'. Is it really true that 'all narratives are capable of darkness' and that 'the oracular is always there'? It is notable that, apart from a few sentences on *Madame Bovary*, the only novelists discussed are Henry James, James Joyce, Henry Green, and Thomas Pynchon. Is *Tom Jones* or *The Heart of Midlothian* or *Pride and Prejudice* or *Middlemarch* 'capable of darkness'? I think even Kermode's ingenuity would find it difficult to find the 'oracular' there, although Douglas Bush performed this feat with his article on 'Mrs. Bennet and the Dark Gods', which some readers accepted as seriously meant.[25]

What troubles me most in the whole exercise is the absence of any literary response to Mark's Gospel. The only place where this occurs is in the brief account of Jean Starobinski's analysis of the cure of the Gerasene demoniac. He is content to write of the story as it appears in the Gospels, without attempting to assimilate or use the attempts of scholars to discover what the original form or point of the story may have been. He treats it as a narrative rather than as a report of an event. His point of entry into the 'hermeneutic circle' is the injunction to the madman to proclaim his cure. 'The demoniac is able to do so because he no longer yells and shrieks but rationally announces. From his freedom—a freedom to be naked among the tombs, and to scream, *une liberté pour rien*—he passes to the constraints of clothes, houses and proclamation.' Starobinski sees this as an example of what an 'outsider' may see which escapes professional exegetes.[26] But I do not feel as I read this that I am listening to either an 'outsider' or an 'insider', but to a sensitive reader, making a point that any preacher might well make in a sermon. It seems wholly different, in its concentration on a single remarkable story, from the attempt to find narrative patterns, 'heterodiegetic analepsis, or intercalation, inexplicit figurations and some sense of an algebra, some formal pattern of opposition and contradiction' in the gospel as a whole. Here I do indeed feel an outsider and do not want to be inside. It is, I suppose, something, that we are told by Kermode at the end that 'We know certain things about Mark: We know, for instance, that we cannot treat this gospel as a work of irony or a confidence trick. . . . But we do so only because of what we have been taught. We have acquired fore-understandings which exclude such readings. This is a benefit, no doubt; but the generic forces that confer it may also prematurely limit the possible senses of the work.' This is asking for a mind so open that it cannot ever shut on anything. But minds, like doors and mouths, are made to shut as well as to open. This is to want the *liberté pour rien* of the demoniac, and prefer such total freedom to the constraints of rational and social intercourse with one's fellow men, through which we discover our true individuality, and grow in knowledge of ourselves, and of the world we find ourselves in.

The only check Kermode appears to see as restraining an endless proliferation of possible meanings is what he refers to many times as 'institutional control'. So to the science of linguistics which makes of men and women mere vehicles rather than users of language, carriers rather than creators, and to forms of analysis that find in literature only endless forms of binary opposition, which can be found just as well in limericks, television advertisements, or graffiti in underground lavatories as in *Paradise Lost* or the Gospel of Mark, sociology is added, and we are controlled by institutional prejudices. On the one side we have insiders whose interpretations are checked by institutional control, believers who approach the gospel with a fore-understanding or prejudice that it has something of importance to say; on the other there is something called 'the institution controlling literary interpretations'. But all this 'institution' seems to do is to 'think well of *Ulysses*', and to be shocked when Robert Adams refuses to bother himself with what Kermode rightly describes as 'the drab enigma' of the 'man in the macintosh', and dares to say that he thinks 'we may be excused for feeling that the fewer answers we have for the novel's riddles the better off we are'.[27] I had thought, when I first met the word 'institution', I was going to find a contrast between churches and universities, but I find myself with an 'in-group' of persons within the literary departments of some universities, who can hardly be regarded as an institution.

For sociological analysis we must, I suppose, call churches and universities institutions; but this is not how they feel, or should feel, to those who are within them. Both, if living organisms and not mere structures for analysis, are communities of persons professing a common faith, with a principle of unity that admits of wide possibilities of diversity, and both bear relations to the societies in which they exist. A university is a community engaged in a common enterprise of advancing and disseminating knowledge, and it lives by its faith in the value and importance of this enterprise. It exists to promote the fruitful intercourse of minds with minds, and is bound together by the respect its members feel for each other's contribution to the common end. We may not understand the finer points of our colleagues' research, but we are aware of its general direction, and there is no lack today of scientists of eminence and authority capable of lucid exposition of the work they do and of its general implications, which can be read with interest and pleasure by any educated person. It used to be thought that it was the distinction of the humanities that they were, more than the sciences, open to all: *Candidae sunt januae Musarum*: the doors of the Muses are open to all is an old adage. But, as has been recently pointed out by a Professor of English Literature, the literary criticism that is regarded by some as most important and innovative to-day is written in a style that is impenetrable to any outside the charmed circle of its practitioners, and, although it has been practised for more than a decade, has not percolated down from academic circles, even in a simplified and vulgarized form, to the general educated public. Outside journals of small circulation, read largely by its practitioners, structuralist, deconstructionist, post-structuralist books are either not reviewed at all, or are reviewed with bafflement, derision, or polite irony.[28] If we are to use the term 'insider' at all, it is they who are the 'insiders'—initiates, inhabitants of a new Laputa, unconcerned with the needs of the society that supports them, and that looks to its universities for the refreshment, reinvigoration, and stimulation of its intellectual life. I have no wish to decry the study of linguistics or of sociology in universities, but I wish to defend the discipline of literary study, or humane letters, from being taken over by these alien disciplines. I have no wish to decry the trying out of new methods and new approaches, if their very limited applicability is recognized. Perhaps I was right to feel obscurely that this was the true point of Kermode's enterprise: that by an eclectic use of different analytical approaches, he ended by displaying their complete inadequacy to deal with the main text to which he was attempting to apply his powers of divination. At least, against the post-structuralists, he is affirming that texts have meaning, although, by affirming that the possibilities they offer to the interpreter are infinite, he is taking away from us any possibilities of agreement on their meaning.

Leaving aside all questions of historicity and of origins, and all the legitimate enquiries of 'higher criticism', surely to any reader, whether atheist, agnostic, or believer, the Gospel of Mark is a marvellous text. Although it is shot through and through with the praeternatural, it does not present us with a world of fairy-tale or fantasy. It presents men and women, some named and some anonymous, who push their way through, or emerge from, jostling crowds, with their needs and their griefs, and their questions, or who engage in brief dialogues. It is full also of brief stories that again deal with men and women engaged in the daily business of living, some foolish, some wise, some harsh, some loving, in their relation with their fellow men. When I complained that typological analysis diminished the 'force and actuality' of the Gospels, I was not complaining that it diminished their 'historicity'; but that it ignored their presentation of a world that reflects the world of human experience. What is at issue here is the whole question of the relation of imaginative literature to the world of human actions, and of the human conscience, a world in which our spiritual and intellectual life is inextricably bound up with our relation to our fellow men, that is with our moral life.

Kermode treats the parables as enigmas, puzzles to be solved, or riddles to be decoded, and finally regards the whole Gospel as an enigma, which may, or possibly may not, have at its heart some esoteric secret. At the beginning of his book he takes as paradigmatic Christ's words to his disciples when they asked him to explain to them the parable of the sower, quoting them in the Revised Standard Version: 'To you has been given the secret of the kingdom of God, but for those outside everything is in parables; so that they may indeed see but not perceive, and may indeed hear but not understand, lest they should turn again and be forgiven' (Mark 4:11–12). He adds that 'perhaps "parables" should be "riddles"'. Tyndale, as well as using the word 'parable', also rendered the Greek word *parabolē* by 'similitude', which seems to me nearer to what the parables, as a literary form, are than either 'riddle' or 'enigma'. They have more of the suggestiveness of metaphor or simile than the form of a puzzle or a riddle, which requires an unequivocal answer and once it is solved loses all interest. For 'secret' the old Revised Version retained the Authorized Version's rendering of the Greek *musterion* as 'mystery'. It is a favourite word with Paul, who uses it constantly, most tellingly at the close of the epistle to the Romans, where he speaks of 'the revelation of the mystery which hath been kept in silence through times eternal but now is manifested' (RV). Christ, as Kermode tells us later, was here using words that Isaiah had heard in the vision that gave him his prophetic mission; or, not to beg the historical question, by placing these words in the mouth of Christ, Mark places him in the historic tradition of the Hebrew prophets. The words express the Hebrew conception of an 'elect', a 'people of God', a 'faithful remnant', which is inseparable from the Hebrew insistence, so alien to Greek thought, on the primacy of the will: the will of God and the wills of men. The Biblical stress on the sovereignty of God and the moral freedom of men must imply, since choice is the instrument of the will, the possibility of refusal and rejection.

In his final chapters Kermode more than once uses the word 'mystery', as if he recognized some difference between it and 'enigma', 'puzzle' or 'secret'. He writes that 'Peter blunders into mystery' in his 'prime recognition of the Messiah'.[29] He uses the same word in speaking of the Transfiguration and its 'ironies—the conjunction of revealed mystery . . . and the silliness of Peter. . . . Mystery and stupidity make an important conjunction or opposition'. He finds the same conjunction and opposition when he comes to the angel at the tomb, who 'proclaims': 'This mystery is confronted with stupid silence.' His comment is revealing: 'We are most unwilling to accept mystery, what cannot be reduced to other more intelligible forms. Yet that is what we find here: something irreducible, therefore perpetually to be interpreted; not secrets to be found out one by one, but Secrecy.'[30] Even with a capital given to it I cannot equate 'mystery', in the admirable definition that Kermode gives of it as 'something irreducible', with 'secrecy'; and anything that is truly 'irreducible' cannot be interpreted, although it can be lived with, and find verification in experience. I think my final dissatisfaction with Kermode's book, for all its incidental virtues, is in his overvaluing of the role of the interpreter, which leads him to his final cheerless conclusion that books, like the world, are 'hopelessly plural, endlessly disappointing'.

It seems a most extraordinary conclusion for anyone to come to who has spent his life in reading and studying literature. Far from being a source of disappointment, it is one of the pleasures of the study of literature, as of teaching it, that great books are inexhaustible. A question from a quite ignorant pupil, who has been really moved, excited, or engaged by the work being discussed, can alter, call in question, open up, the sense or meaning of the whole, so that was familiar becomes once again 'wonderful'. If it were really possible for 'interpretation' to arrive at a final, completely adequate interpretation of the 'meaning' of an imaginative text, or fiction, the text would no longer be worth reading. Its meaning must always lie beyond an interpreter's power, if it is to retain its power over the imagination of its readers. The interpreter can cast light here or there, supply 'radiancies', as indeed intermittently Kermode does, but he can never become the text's master.

NOTES

1 *The Limits of Literary Criticism* (Oxford, 1956), the Riddell Memorial Lectures for that year; republished in *The Business of Criticism* (Oxford, 1959).
2 *The Sense of an Ending* (New York, 1957), 48.
3 *Modern Language Notes* (1969), 891–915.
4 The Eliot Memorial Lectures for 1973 (published London, 1975).
5 pp. 18–20.
6 p. 37.
7 See particularly Beryl Smalley, *The Study of the Bible in the Middle Ages* (Oxford, 1952).
8 p. 107.
9 p. 111.
10 p. 82.
11 p. 98.
12 p. 138.
13 p. 127.
14 The classic Byzantine scheme for the decoration of churches did not include the rising from the tomb or any Resurrection appearances. The Crucifixion was followed by the Descent into Hell, the *anastasis* being represented by the *katabasis*. The narrative ended here, and the eye then moved to Christ in glory. The two most impressive representations in art of the Resurrection that I have seen are Piero della Francesca's of Christ rising from the tomb, and a fresco by an unknown artist at Milesova in Jugoslavia. This shows simply the angel seated at the side of the tomb, pointing to the empty grave-clothes.
15 p. 83.
16 p. 96.
17 pp. 117 and 160, nn. 25 and 26.
18 Oxford Society of Historical Theology, *Abstract of Proceedings for the Academic Year, 1950–60*, printed for private circulation. I am a little distressed by Kermode's statement that Austin Farrer's work was 'rejected by the establishment, and eventually by himself, largely because it was too literary. The institution knew intuitively that such literary elaboration . . . was unacceptable because damaging to what remained of the idea that the gospel narratives were still, in some measure, transparent upon history' (p. 63). I know of no means by which the 'establishment' or the 'institution', by which I assume is meant the

Church of England, 'rejects' views. It appears to many to be conspicuously feeble in not doing so. And Austin Farrer was a man of complete intellectual honesty. He modified, without 'rejecting', his views after further study of Mark in relation to Matthew.

19 A famous example is Mark 2:10, where the awkward syntax is exactly reproduced in both Matthew and Luke, more elegant writers than Mark, who have not, as we would expect, cleaned it up.

20 p. 113.

21 Divinity Moderations was an examination which all candidates for the degree of BA at Oxford had to pass in order to qualify for the degree. In Wilde's time the texts set for study from the New Testament were in Greek. When Greek was no longer compulsory for entrance to the university, four Gospels and Acts in English, or one Gospel and Acts in Greek were set. The examination, now abolished, led to considerable ribaldry, particularly in the mnemonics devised for helping with the missionary journeys of Paul, handed down by seniors to juniors.

22 *Son of Oscar Wilde* (London, 1954), 25–6.

23 p. 114.

24 This anecdote was brought to my notice by Andrew Wilson.

25 First published in the *New Statesman*, reprinted in *Engaged and Disengaged* (Cambridge, Mass., 1966).

26 Kermode is quoting from a text in *Analyse structurale et exégèse biblique* by R. Barthes and Others (Paris, 1971). There is another version in Jean Starobinski, *Trois Fureurs* (Paris, 1974), with the title 'Le Combat avec Légion', which is translated in *New Literary History*, (1973), 4, where a note states that it was originally delivered as a lecture to the Faculty of Theology of the University of Geneva.

27 pp. 52–3. See Robert M. Adams, *Surface and Symbol* (New York, 1962), 165, 218, 245–6.

28 See David Lodge, 'Structural Defects', *Observer*, 23 March 1980: 'As an academic critic and university teacher specialising in modern literature and literary theory, I spend much of my time these days reading books and articles that I can barely understand and that cause my wife (a graduate with a good honours degree in English language and literature) to utter loud cries of pain and nausea if her eyes happen to fall on them. At the same time I am uncomfortably aware that literary criticism no longer has the prestige it once enjoyed in our culture at large. These two facts are not unconnected. The most important, trail-blazing criticism now being produced is written in a style that is impenetrable to the layman. To paraphrase Yeats, the most readable critics lack all conviction and the least are full of passionate intensity.'

29 p. 115.

30 pp. 142–3.

Chapter VI

Apologia Pro Vita Mea

Just as I was about to fly out to Harvard in October 1979 I was given an advance copy of a collection of essays on the literature of the English Renaissance by former pupils and colleagues, which I brought out with me with great pride and pleasure.[1] The editor, in a very kind preface, explained that if the tributes collected had matched the variety of the items in my bibliography printed at the end of the volume, the collection would have been wholly miscellaneous, and it was therefore decided to restrict the topics treated to English Literature of the late sixteenth and seventeenth centuries. This was prudent, for publishers have to sell books, and want to feel that there is a possible public for a book before they accept it. It was also right, because this period is 'my home of love'. However much and however happily I have ranged elsewhere, I always feel I have come home when I return to what is to me the most inexhaustible and the most deeply pleasurable of all periods of our poetry.

I have to own that my bibliography looks rather like a synopsis of one of the more tangled sections in the middle of *The Faerie Queene* or the *Orlando Furioso*, with subjects, like Ariosto's knights or ladies, disappearing for a while to turn up later, or else to sink forever out of sight, and new, unexpected ones surfacing for a moment. And yet, although I have not yet done what I set out long ago to do, and perhaps now never shall, I feel with Spenser that I have not lost my 'compasse' and that, though my course has often been 'stayd', it has never really been 'astray'. Looking back, my career is a story of opportunities offered, of chances and lucky accidents deflecting me from what I was planning to do, of problems encountered in teaching, which I could not resist giving attention to, of invitations that it seemed cowardly to refuse, and of what had seemed a blind alley that I had turned back from unexpectedly joining up with new paths. I might have done better if I had had, like

Socrates, a daemon that said to me 'No'. My daemon has always said to me 'Yes', and my guide through the 'delightful land of Poesy' has been a search for pleasure, for pleasures of every kind, so that I would echo Spenser's words, as he began on his sixth book:

> The waies, through which my weary steps I guyde,
> In this delightful land of Poesy,
> Are so exceeding spacious and wyde,
> And sprincled with such sweet variety,
> Of all that pleasant is to eare and eye,
> That I nigh rauist with rare thoughts delight,
> My tedious travell doe forget thereby;
> And when I gin to feel decay of might,
> It strength to me supplies, and chears my dulled spright.

It was in my last year at school, where I had a remarkable English mistress, that I found where my true home was, and I was told that I won my scholarship at St. Hilda's College, Oxford, in 1926 by my answers on Shakespeare, Donne, and Milton. At Oxford I read what was then the ordinary course for English Honours, working for three 'language' and six literature papers. As a reward for obtaining a first class in 1929 the London County Council, which had paid for my education from the age of eleven to twenty-one,[2] gave me an extension of my scholarship for one further year. The obvious thing to have done would have been to have looked for a subject for a B.Litt. that I could have broken the back of in my one year, and, as only one year of residence for the degree was necessary for an Oxford graduate, gone down, found employment, and hoped to find time to finish the thesis in my spare time. In those far-off days prudential considerations did not weigh so heavily on students as they have come to do, and, in any case, it seemed so unlikely that I should ever have the chance to become a teacher in a university that the thought of using this priceless extra year just to get a second degree as quickly as possible did not occur to me. At this time, in England, the idea that it was quite impossible for anyone to teach in a university, or to attempt to be a scholar and write a book, without a research degree had not cast its dark shadow.

I was very conscious of how totally inadequate my knowledge of medieval literature was, and I had come to feel that if I ever wanted to work on Shakespeare and Donne, my secret ambition, I ought to be better equipped to 'stalk them from behind'. I had no notion that this same idea had struck, and indeed was striking, many people in America as well as in England: that Willard Farnham at Berkeley, who many years later was to become a friend, was at work on *The Medieval Inheritance of Elizabethan Tragedy*, and that a rather solemn young man, whom I was later to meet taking a class on the text of *Comus* for the probationer B.Litts., in place of Percy Simpson, was shortly to produce *The Allegory of Love*. Thinking myself a lone pioneer, instead of a belated recruit to a growing army, I asked Dorothy Everett, with whom I had done my medieval work as an undergraduate, for help in finding a subject to work on in the fourteenth century. She had liked the work I had done for her on the Yorkshire mystic Richard Rolle, whom she had worked on at Cambridge, and directed me towards what was then virtually virgin soil, the later fourteenth-century mystics: the author of *The Cloud of Unknowing*, Walter Hilton, and Julian of Norwich. Apart from Evelyn Underhill, who had written on them and published some of their works in modernized texts, and some Catholic scholars, who had published some works, also in modern texts, for the old Orchard Series, the only worker in the field was Hope Emily Allen, most devoted and generous of scholars, whose massive *Writings Ascribed to Richard Rolle and Materials for his Biography* had appeared in 1927. I set out in total ignorance to investigate the canon of Walter Hilton; but decided after a term that what was really needed was a text of his classic work *The Scale of Perfection* of which his authorship was unquestioned. I settled down to hunting for manuscripts of this long work, in the original English and in its Latin translation, and then to the awesome task of collating them. Meanwhile, I also plunged into the Fathers in the attempt to track down Hilton's sources. I was so naïve that I thought that this canon of a not very distinguished Augustinian house read the Fathers *in extenso*, and I spent long hours in the Selden end of the Bodleian standing by the shelves that housed Migne's *Patrologia*, as it was easier to heave the volume onto the ledge above and read it standing than to carry it back to a seat and fix it up on a reading desk. I did not realize that Hilton's frequent quotations from Gregory and other notable Latin Fathers most probably came from a *Flores Patrum*. Although I do not think that toiling through the execrably printed double columns of Migne was very good for my eyesight, or for my Latinity, I do not think my time was wholly wasted. Like many people I owe much to the Abbé Migne's splendid analytical indexes; but I am glad I was not at this stage content to be one of the 'Ferrets and Moushunts of an Index',[3] but gained at least some acquaintance with the methods of Biblical exegesis, and with the minds of Augustine, Gregory, and Bernard.

At the same time I followed the special courses provided for the little group of ten or twelve students for the B.Litt. in English: David Nichol Smith on the history of English scholarship, Percy Simpson on Elizabethan Handwriting and Textual Problems, and Strickland Gibson on Bibliography. Since I was working on a medieval subject, I was allowed to join a class of History students on medieval Latin palaeography conducted by the great E. A. Lowe. This was one of the happiest years of my life: the only year in which I had nothing to do but read in the Bodleian and attend these classes, where we were taken seriously as persons wanting to enter the community of scholars, and felt pride when Dr Lowe, after he had asked if anyone could read a certain word and someone had boldly attempted to do so, might say: 'A good guess; but you could make it better'; or Percy Simpson, after a long pause in which he reflected on a pupil's attempt to defend a colon in the second quarto of *Romeo and Juliet*, would shake his finger with a solemn warning: 'Yes; but if you are not careful, you *might* turn into another Dover Wilson.'

Most research scholarships at this time were offered by the colleges, and the women's colleges were not rich in them. There was one that was open to women only, which I applied for and was awarded. It would not have provided me with enough to live on; but I thought I could find ways of supplementing it. Just as I was about to return to Oxford after the long vacation for a second year of research, I received a telegram from Ernest de Selincourt, Professor of English at Birmingham, asking me whether I could come at short notice to take the place of a member of his staff who wanted leave of absence to nurse a sick mother. He had, as he usually did, turned to his old friend Helen Darbishire of Somerville, to ask her to recommend a Somervillian. She, by a remarkable stroke of luck for me, had not got one available, and told him that there was a young woman at St. Hilda's who was well spoken of, and gave him my name. At this time, the autumn of 1930, the chance of my ever obtaining a university post seemed remote. I had applied for a few and had not even had my references taken up. So, although it was only for one term, I had no hesitation in giving up my award and wiring acceptance to de Selincourt. I kept on my lodgings at Oxford and went up to Birmingham for three days a week to give tutorials to students reading for Honours and to take an Adult Education class. At half-term de Selincourt sent for me and asked me whether I was willing to stay on for a second term, as the person I was replacing had asked for an extension of leave. Disguising my exultation at the prospect of the wolf being kept from the door for another term, I said I should be happy to do so. De Selincourt's backing was, of course, very powerful, and, with it, I applied for a post at Royal Holloway College, University of London, and was appointed to an assistant lectureship for three years. At the end of my time, a post fell vacant at Birmingham. I taught at Birmingham for seven very happy years until 1941, when I returned to my own old college at Oxford as a tutorial fellow.

At London, Birmingham, and Oxford, I followed the English pattern of that time of teaching undergraduates the whole range of English Literature from Chaucer to wherever the syllabus stopped. But up to the outbreak of war in 1939 I continued to toil away at *The Scale of Perfection*, collecting shoe-box after shoe-box stuffed with variant readings, and spending much of my spare time in general medieval and theological reading. The enterprise was more and more remote from my teaching, and from the reading I was doing for it and for my lectures. It seemed more and more inappropriate, as the troubled thirties grew more and more troubled, to the circumstances of my life. Like most of my generation I was passionately involved in politics, both domestic and foreign. Birmingham, which it was said was still living on the profits of the last war when it began to benefit from the preparations for the next one, presented the strange spectacle of a large industrial town in which all twelve constituencies were held by Conservatives. I spent a great deal of my time canvassing for the Labour Party in the working-class areas of Edgbaston, Neville Chamberlain's constituency, and, after the outbreak of the Spanish Civil War, in organizing meetings and collecting money in the Midlands in aid of the Spanish Republicans. Later there were Red Cross classes in First Aid and training classes for air-raid wardens to fit in, as preparation for a war that began to seem inevitable. When war came the manuscripts of the British Museum went underground; but for the six years of war, even if manuscripts had still been available, there seemed more urgent tasks for an able-bodied person to perform than editing *The Scale of Perfection*, and more urgent professional duties: to try to keep human values alive in a world that seemed to be relapsing into barbarism. To be able to go on teaching in such a world was a great comfort, and I think it was the experience of these years that confirmed my faith in the renovating power of the literature of past ages. Long before the war ended I knew that I could not go back to work on Hilton. I was not prepared to make myself a good enough philologist to cope with the linguistic problems involved. More important, I had come to doubt the possibility of arriving by the classical methods of textual analysis at a satisfactory text of a vernacular prose work, written for edification, and copied by scribes who spoke different dialects, and either incorporated into the text glosses they found in the manuscript they were copying, or glossed it themselves. It did not seem probable that Hilton's book would repay the heroic solution the Early English Text Society had arrived at with *Ancrene Wisse*, of editing each of the extant manuscripts separately instead of attempting to produce a definitive text.[4] So far, what I have said about my professional career sounds like a lamentable tale of wasted energy and misdirected enthusiasm.[5]

To return to Birmingham. In the spring of 1940, during the period described as the 'phoney war', Keith Hancock, then Professor of History, organized a series of lunch-hour lectures in the old building in the centre of the city in which the Faculty of Arts was still working. They were half-hour talks, for the benefit of persons working in the vicinity, on current problems, economic and political: for instance, there was one on the law of blockade, and whether we were justified in seizing the *Altmark* in Norwegian territorial waters. The lectures were very well attended by people bringing in their sandwiches and enjoying a half-hour of clear and authoritative exposition. I said to Hancock, half as a joke, that I thought the citizens of Birmingham needed perhaps something more enlivening to help them endure the long hours of black-out, which had brought social life virtually to an end. Many of them had dutifully made their way through *War and Peace*, which had been recommended by E. M. Forster and others as a good read at the beginning of the conflict. It was seen everywhere, in buses, and the London Tube, and in restaurants where office workers took their lunches. I thought people might be grateful for some further suggestions. He took up the idea and approached the acting-head of the English Department, but had no success there. He came back to me and said that I had better do it, as it was my idea. My daemon, as always, said to me: 'Say yes.' I offered to give three lectures in the summer term on 'A Victorian Novelist', 'A Modern Novelist', and 'A Modern Poet'. I decided to recommend Trollope, particularly what are now called 'The Palliser Chronicles'; Graham Greene, particularly *The Power and the Glory*; and T. S. Eliot.

Eliot may seem to have been an odd choice to recommend to Birmingham business men and office workers as good wartime reading. The reason I chose him was that, coming home one day in late March to my Birmingham bed-sitting-

room, I had found a packet. It had been sent to me by
Henry Reed, a former graduate student at Birmingham,
who was at this time gathering the experiences that led to
'Naming of Parts', perhaps the best English poem that came
out of the second world war, as a private soldier. He was
later to write the best parody of Eliot's later manner:
'Chard Whitlow', beginning 'As we grow older we do not
grow any younger'. The packet contained the Easter
Supplement to the *New English Weekly*, an obscure periodical, which contained a new poem by Eliot, *East Coker*. I
shall never forget my first reading of this poem on that
dreary day in late March 1940. It was the most dispiriting
period of the war. We had nerved ourselves to endure
hideous calamities. All we got was impotence, when Poland,
on whose behalf we had declared war, was destroyed in a
few weeks, a stalemate on the Western Front, the brief
episode of the war between Russia and Finland, the bungled
débâcle of Norway, the endless boredom of the black-out
and of press and radio propaganda, with a government in
charge in which it was impossible to have any confidence.
The attempt to build a Popular Front against Fascism and
Nazism had collapsed with the Nazi–Soviet pact. People I
had worked with and trusted were now saying that the war
was a capitalist war, and a 'phoney war' at that. Alas, this
was exactly what it felt like. Along with other younger
members of the staff of the university, I had accepted a call
to go out once a week to talk to isolated groups of 'old
sweats' (reservists called back to the colours) and young
recruits, who were stranded in Nissen huts in the country-
side around Birmingham manning anti-aircraft posts to
protect the Ham Hall power-station. We were an odd
collection, a clergyman who did conjuring tricks, a ven-
triloquist, and a group of university lecturers who were
supposed to deal with 'current affairs'. I was asked to talk
about the press and help my hearers to follow the news. My
task, as I conceived it, was to persuade them not to believe
everything they read in the papers; but I rapidly discovered
this was quite unnecessary, as they did not believe anything
at all. Instead, I had to persuade them that some things were
true, were really happening, and were not just propaganda. I

found myself in the presence of a good-humoured, bottom-less, and perhaps, I feared, justified cynicism. Reading *East Coker* for the first time on that late March afternoon, I found myself reading a poem that offered no easy comfort, but only the true comfort of hearing a voice speaking out of the darkness without cynicism and without despair. By the time I came to give my lecture, the balloon had at last gone up, and there was no doubt at all that things were happening. I talked about the poem for a quarter of an hour and then read it. It was plain by the absolute silence with which it was listened to that it spoke to the condition of many present as it spoke to mine. When in February 1941 *The Dry Salvages* appeared in the same periodical, a group of young people, poets, painters, journalists, and former under-graduates, asked me to talk to them about it, and afterwards urged me to publish something on these poems. I wrote an article on 'The Recent Poetry of T. S. Eliot' and sent it to Cyril Connolly for *Horizon*. It must have lain for some time unread on his desk, as I realized from its virgin state when, at my request, he sent it back to me. I sent it to John Lehmann who published it in a short-lived wartime publi-cation called *Daylight and New Writing* where it appeared in 1942. I did not realize that another poem was to follow, and, after *Little Gidding* appeared, I revised the article, at Lehmann's request, for his paperback *Penguin New Writing* and also for a collection of essays on Eliot, where it appeared in 1947. I thought that was the end of that.

In 1941 I heard from my old college at Oxford that my tutor was retiring, and was asked whether I would like to apply for the post. I felt very uncertain what to do. Although Birmingham was not one of the most heavily bombed cities, it was being heavily bombed. The lecture theatre in which I had given my lectures was wrecked, and we were teaching in what rooms were left, nipping down to the cellars with our pupils when the German planes returned in the morning to photograph what damage they had done. It was rumoured that Oxford was never going to be bombed. One story was that there was an agreement that Oxford would be spared if Nuremberg was; another was that Hitler wanted Oxford as the Headquarters of the Nazi

Youth Movement. I have no idea what truth, if any, there was in these rumours; but it is true that no bombs fell in Oxford and that Cambridge had only one stick, which was dropped by a pilot off his course and anxious to shed his load. To leave Birmingham for the shelter of Oxford seemed a kind of desertion. More important was the fact that I knew by now that I was a good teacher and that I loved teaching: I had no certainty that I should ever be a scholar, if by a scholar is meant not a person with a certain habit of mind but a person who makes a recognized contribution to knowledge by publication. I had published three articles on a subject that I knew I could not go on with, and an article on the Nunnery scene in *Hamlet* looked at in the light of the conventions governing overhearing in Shakespeare's other plays. Another consideration was that I had tasted residential life in my three years at Royal Holloway College and had no desire to go back to it. I had greatly enjoyed working in a university in a large industrial city and making friends outside the academic community. So, I hesitated. I had almost decided not to apply, when I received a letter from my old supervisor, Dorothy Everett, urging me to apply and giving reasons that made her sure that it would be wrong of me not to do so. I have always had great sympathy with Donne in his expressions of gratitude to King James for making him take holy orders. I realize now that Dorothy Everett knew me much better than I knew myself.

The Oxford that I went back to was a strange Oxford with most of the younger dons either in the forces or seconded to various wartime ministries. Almost all the young men, and many of the young women, were doing short courses while waiting for their call-up. It meant a heavy and complicated teaching-load; but this was nothing compared with the situation when the war ended and Oxford had to accommodate both those whose careers had been interrupted by the war and the young coming up from school—with depleted faculties, for the ministries were slow to release their temporary civil servants, buildings still requisitioned, and a terrible shortage of lodgings. At Birmingham, although I had taught Donne in tutorials, lectures on Donne were the preserve of my colleague I. A. Shapiro, then, as now, engaged in editing Donne's letters. At Oxford, lectures are not the main mode of instruction, and, whereas at Birmingham lecture courses were arranged and topics allocated, at Oxford the lecture list, particularly in English, presented a pleasing chaos of offerings that the students could attend, or absent themselves from, at choice. (I have never decided whether having a captive audience, which could display its displeasure by cat-calls, hooting, stamping, or sleeping, or one that, as at Oxford, could 'fold their tents, like the Arabs, and as silently steal away', is the severer test of a lecturer.) Some research into past lecture lists showed me that very few courses had been given on the Metaphysicals, and nobody, for some time, had given a course on Donne alone. I set to work to prepare lectures on Donne and on the Metaphysicals. Early in 1946, returning from a lecture, I slipped on a patch of ice and found myself in cap and gown, with a pile of books under my arm, sitting on the pavement in the Broad with my right foot at right angles with my leg. Oxford is tolerant of eccentricity, and for a while I sat there quietly until a young man and his wife stopped and asked if I needed help. He called a couple of undergraduates, told them to kneel down and hold me firmly round the back to support me, and there and then reduced a classic Potts fracture. I was got into a taxi, sent to hospital, put into a plaster, told that I must not put the foot to the ground for six weeks, and sent back to college. The Librarian called in to commiserate and told me that Parker's Catalogue was offering a copy of Donne's *LXXX Sermons* for fourteen pounds. Did I want it? She telephoned for me, went and fetched the book, and that evening it lay upon my lap. The booksellers had not collated it, and it had one gathering missing. They had also not noticed that it contained not only the *LXXX Sermons* of 1640 but also the *L Sermons* of 1650. I had one hundred and thirty sermons of Donne to read at home in college during six weeks in which I had nothing else to do except give tutorials. I settled down to read the sermons through and to supplement from them Grierson's commentary on the poems. I found that Donne, usually so cautious in settling doctrinal points, again and again recurred with a curious insistence to a certain theological point, on which, while owning that the Fathers were in dispute here, he declared that 'we had now arrived at certainty'. I saw that, for the line in one of the 'Holy Sonnets' for which I had collected all these passages in the sermons, and which expressed the same view, there existed a variant in several manuscripts in which Donne expressed uncertainty. It seemed he had at some moment changed his mind. As soon as I was able to get back to Bodley I set to work to write a long article on 'The Date, Order, and Interpretation of the "Holy Sonnets" of John Donne'. I was wondering where to send it, when Hugo Dyson of Merton and his wife came to dinner with me in college. Being full of the subject I started to tell him about it. With his usual warmth and generosity he thought it fascinating and exclaimed: 'Don't put it in an article. Nobody reads articles. Why not produce an edition? Then we can have the poems there to refer to while we read what you want to say.' I realized that an edition of nineteen sonnets would hardly commend itself to a publisher, and as I had collected a great deal of material on Donne's 'Litany', which I had always admired and thought that Grierson and others had undervalued, the idea of editing the *Divine Poems* came into my mind and I wrote to the Clarendon Press to ask if it could be considered. Kenneth Sisam, the then Secretary, who was about to retire, and Dan Davin, who was to take over responsibility for the bulk of the academic publishing, interviewed me. After I had put my case, which was kindly received, I added: 'I suppose I may treat Grierson's text as the *textus receptus*, and concentrate on the introduction and commentary.' Sisam said mildly that he thought I ought to 'take a look at Grierson's text'. Here I was back again hunting down manuscripts and collating them. At least I did not have to be an expert in Middle English dialects; and the text was in verse, which provided some check on the variants. Sisam added that Dr Paul Maas was now in Oxford and was assisting the Press on textual matters, and he thought I would be well advised to consult him. This was an awe-inspiring suggestion, as Maas was, I suppose, now that Housman was dead, the greatest living classical textual scholar. When I finally sent him my text and textual notes for comment, he went over the material with scrupulous care and kindness, although, like most classical scholars, he was baffled by our fuss over old spelling and the original punctuation. I had the pleasure of giving a short lecture on elementary bibliography to this great man. He listened with the utmost courtesy and politeness but without being convinced.

I soon found myself in a difficulty. The Dowden manuscript of Donne's poems was in the possession of a certain Mr Wilfred Merton, who also possessed the Dowden manuscript of some of Donne's sermons. Evelyn Simpson told me that she had written to him to ask whether she might see the manuscript of the sermons and had had no reply. She told me that she had heard that he was a recluse and did not answer letters. The Dowden manuscript of the poems was a very important manuscript and, if I were to examine Grierson's handling of the text, I had to see it. I thought I had better not risk a direct application to the owner but should try an indirect approach. John Hayward had used it for his Nonesuch edition of Donne's *Poems and Selected Prose* in 1929, so I wrote to him, out of the blue, to ask him if he could give me any help in approaching the reluctant owner. He replied that he could not remember how he had got access; but that he thought Evelyn Simpson was wrongly informed, and gave me Wilfred Merton's address. It turned out that Evelyn Simpson *was* wrongly informed and I received a most kind and prompt reply to my letter, with an offer to deposit both manuscripts in the Bodleian for Evelyn Simpson's and my use. This was another extraordinary piece of good fortune. But for Evelyn Simpson's error I should never have written to John Hayward. He added at the close of his letter to me that, although he was afraid he could not help me, he would like to meet me as he had admired my article on *Four Quartets*, and invited me to come and have tea. Although I knew that Eliot and Hayward shared a flat at this time, my letter was quite innocent of any intention of making contact with the poet through his friend, and I accepted the invitation thinking it would be a merely social occasion. I arrived, as bidden, at 4.30 and I think I did not leave until around 7.30. During the course of conversation Hayward, who was a cripple and tied to his desk in a wheelchair, told me to go to the bookshelf and get down a slim volume labelled 'Little Gidding'. It contained a typescript of the first draft of the poem, typescripts of Eliot's revisions, and letters of Eliot to Hayward commenting on Hayward's criticisms. This was the beginning of a close and rewarding friendship. Whenever I was in London I would go to tea with Hayward and soon Eliot would call in around 5.30 on his return from Faber's for half-an-hour's pleasant, desultory chat. I never spoke to him about his poetry, or asked him any questions. We talked of affairs, Oxford gossip, and literary matters in general—about anything that came up, except his poetry.

At the end of the war David Nichol Smith retired from the Merton Chair of English Literature and F. P. Wilson was elected to succeed him. He was determined that Oxford in general, and Merton College in particular, should no longer continue their disgraceful refusal to recognize that they had harboured, although only for one year, a great poet. So, at last, Eliot was given an Hon. D.Litt. by the university, and elected to an honorary fellowship at Merton. Emboldened by this, I asked Wilson whether he thought the Board of the Faculty would accept four lectures by me on Eliot on the lecture list, as an additional offering to the lectures I was giving on the syllabus. He welcomed the idea and I put down four lectures for the spring of 1948. In London over Christmas, I rang up Hayward and arranged to go to tea on 1 January 1948. I read in the morning papers of that day that the King had awarded Eliot the Order of Merit, the highest honour in the sovereign's personal gift. After tea, as usual, Eliot called in and I congratulated him, and we had our usual pleasant talk. As I was leaving, with the rather ironic tone I often adopted to him, I said 'This is your *Annus Mirabilis*: the King has given you the OM and your name is appearing on the Oxford lecture list. I am giving four lectures on you next term.' To which he replied, with his usual tone of grave consideration: 'Well, perhaps better you than some.'[6] As I went out of the door, Hayward swivelled round from his desk and called out: 'Why don't you make them into a book and let the Cresset Press publish it?' On the bus back from Chelsea to Highgate the idea seemed more and more attractive and on getting home I telephoned Hayward and said: 'I shall call it "The Art of T. S. Eliot", and you shall have it by the beginning of the summer.' I laid the *Divine Poems* of John Donne aside for three months, and in the evenings of the spring term, after dinner and late into the night, I wrote away, and sent the typescript to Hayward soon after Easter. Like Wordsworth, speaking of 'The Idiot Boy', I can say that I never wrote anything else 'with so much glee'. Hayward read it with his usual minute care, and then summoned me to what he called 'the stool of repentance' to point out errors and infelicities of expression—'Severe outbreak of "but disease" here', he would say, pointing to a page on which he had ringed a series of 'buts'. It was accepted by the publisher in September and appeared in 1949. It was my first book, and I was forty-one when it appeared. I went back to Donne's *Divine Poems*, which was published in 1952. While I was working on it, Wesley Milgate had arrived in Oxford from Sydney, as the first Nuffield Fellow in the Humanities, to work for three years on Donne, and F. P. Wilson brought us together. It was Wilson's idea that the *Divine Poems* should be the first volume of a four-volume edition of Donne's poems, on the model of the Twickenham edition of Pope.

Now my way seemed clear, and especially after 1954, when, on my return from my first visit to the United States as a Visiting Professor at the University of California at Los Angeles, I was elected to a new Readership in English Renaissance Literature. This had been founded to meet the situation created by the huge increase in the number of graduate students at Oxford. Normally Readers, while like Professors bound to give at least six lecture courses a year, are unlike Professors in that they may, if they wish to, give up to six hours a week in tutorial teaching to under-graduates. But the amount of graduate supervision, teach-ing, and examining was so great, that I had reluctantly to decide I could not, if I meant to go on with work on Donne, find time to go on with undergraduate teaching. The bulk of my lectures was for undergraduates; but I missed the particular pleasures of tutorial teaching. Yet, although I now seemed at last settled in a professional routine, my book on Eliot had brought me new friends, and contacts with a world outside the universities, and invitations—to review, to lecture, and to broadcast on topics that interested me but where I could not claim special expertise. And again I found myself saying 'Yes'. I greatly enjoyed these contacts with what some severer academics, the 'Scrutineers', regarded as the corrupt metropolitan literary world, and the provincial one too. Particularly I enjoyed the four weeks I used to spend during the long vacation on a BBC programme called 'The Critics', where five persons, with a chairman to hold the ring and see fair shares of the time, discussed a new book, a play, a film, an art exhibition, and a radio programme. I was responsible for choosing the book and opening the discussion on it. Sometimes the books offering themselves were not very exciting; but there were great moments, as when *Dr Zhivago* presented itself, and I remember another when I persuaded my, at first, alarmed colleagues, who were later grateful, to let me choose Edgar Wind's *Pagan Mysteries of the Renaissance* for discussion. Wind was overwhelmed with pleasure to hear his book being discussed on a BBC Home Service programme. It was during this period that I was asked by the editor of Penguin Poets to provide them with an anthology of *Metaphysical Poets*. Here, I suppose, I could claim that I was fulfilling the duties of my post, and I know that the book is widely used by undergraduates in universities. But it was not intended to be a textbook, and I am delighted that it is still, after over twenty years, in general circulation.

It was around the same time that I gave the lectures on the interpretation of poetry and Scripture already mentioned. I should hardly have ventured onto this dangerous ground but for the fact that I had been investigating out of pure curiosity a little problem that I had come across on a holiday in Venice. I had been struck and surprised to find on the Doge's palace, on the opposite corner to that on which was carved a representation of the Fall of Man, not, as I expected, a carving of the Crucifixion, but a representation of Noah naked and drunk in his tent, with his two bad sons mocking at their poor old father for being so overcome, and his good son hastening forward with a robe to cover his nakedness. I had travelled a good deal in France before the war and had always been interested in iconography; but I did not visit Italy until after the disappearance of Mussolini. Now I was making up for my abstention. Wherever I went I saw what I had not noticed in my travels in France, representations in mosaics, frescos, and carving of the intoxicated patriarch. There he was inside the atrium of St. Mark's, on the Baptistery doors in Florence, and on the ceiling of the Sistine chapel. I was also pleased to find him on Giotto's campanile, among the benefactors of the human race, as the discoverer of wine 'which maketh glad the heart of man'. I had been investigating the meanings given to this curious and rather improper episode in Genesis, and was interested to find that it had attracted the attention of Simone Weil, who gave it a totally different mystical interpretation from that given by the Fathers. So I had some material at hand which provided me with a first lecture on 'The Drunkenness of Noah'. I delivered this without suggesting any reservations about the current enthusiasm for mystical senses and symbolic images. I was afterwards told that the canons of Durham returned sadly from Newcastle, feeling the world had gone mad, to enjoy what one of them called the best *peripeteia* he had ever experienced the next evening, when, towards the close of a lecture on 'The Poetry of St. Mark', I turned to suggest what seemed to me some serious limitations on this method of arriving at meaning.

This delightful period came to an end in 1961 when the Prime Minister, Harold Macmillan, asked me to serve on a committee on Higher Education under the chairmanship of Lionel Robbins. This involved meetings in London twice a week to hear evidence, journeys abroad, to Switzerland, Sweden, West Germany, France, Holland, the Soviet Union, and the United States, to study their systems and their solutions to the problems caused by the expansion of higher education all over the world. In the United Kingdom expansion was urgently needed to deal not only with the 'bulge' in the post-war birthrate but also with the consequences of the revolutionary Butler Education Act of 1944. The early nineteen-sixties was a period of great optimism. Economists were confidently prophesying steady growth in the Gross National Product, and slogans such as 'I'm all right, Jack' and 'You've never had it so good' expressed a general mood in England. The six new universities were not the result of our report. Sussex was already in being, and the others were in various stages of planning and construction when we began our deliberations.[7] I do not myself think there is any truth in the generally held view that our report lowered standards. Most parents want their children to have more than they had themselves: those who had left school at sixteen wanted their children to stay until eighteen, and those who had stayed at school until eighteen and then gone out into the world wanted their children to go to the university. It seemed probable to our statisticians, extrapolating from present trends, that the steady increase since the war in the numbers in sixth forms, and in those getting good results in their A level examinations, would continue. Unless the number of places was expanded, the universities would progressively be rejecting more and more young people who a few years before they would have been glad to accept. We had overwhelming evidence from the schools that the stiffness of the competition for a place in a university was distorting the curriculum and damaging the teaching in the upper forms of schools. Believing that here 'More' would not mean 'Worse', we recommended that places ought to be provided in the universities for all applicants that the universities themselves thought worthy of admission. I still believe that this was the right recommendation, and my impression is that in my own subject the standard of the average undergraduate has gone up and is higher than it was when I began to teach; and I do not hear many complaints from colleagues about the quality of their students.[8] We ought, perhaps, to have been more aware of the difficulties inherent in a large increase during a short period in the numbers of persons teaching in universities. A great many people came into the profession of roughly the same age, who are going to be there for a long time. If the highly optimistic forecasts that were being made when we were sitting had been justified in the event, this might have meant some loss of opportunity for promotion with a consequent loss of new appointments at the bottom of the ladder. With the disastrous reversal of economic expectations we are now experiencing, the situation has become very serious for some of the ablest of our students. New posts will not be created and those that fall vacant may well have to be either suspended or discontinued.

I feel the greatest sympathy and concern for young graduate students, who are in much the same situation that my generation was in fifty years ago; but their situation is much more bitter because it follows on a period in which a good first degree followed by a period of graduate study, if it did not guarantee, at least made probable the prospect of a career of teaching and research in the universities. Further, I see a time coming when young people, who have spent many years working for a doctorate and then turning their theses into books, are going to find it extremely difficult to publish their work. I am speaking here out of my experience as a Delegate of the Oxford University Press, and in assessing applications for research awards. When I first became a Delegate the sordid topic of money hardly entered into discussions of a proposal or of a book that had been sent to the Press for consideration. By the time I retired, six years ago, it seemed at times that we discussed very little else. Of recent years applications to grant-giving bodies have begun to include more and more requests for assistance towards finding a subsidy demanded by the publisher as a condition of acceptance of a manuscript.

I think we have to recognize that there are lean years ahead for us all, and that the humanities are always in the greatest danger at a time of financial stringency, although this is just the time when their influence is most needed as a source of spiritual strength for society at large. We are going to need all the faith and courage and nerve we have to defend the value of the study of literature. I think this will require a reconsideration of the accepted patterns of the academic study of English literature, and in particular of the value of our present ways of organizing graduate study and what its purpose is. I hope most people would agree with me that the last thirty or so years have seen gross over-production in the field of English literary study. Material that would make a note is blown up into an article, and material that would make an article is extended into a book, by indulging in discussion of all previous work on the subject whether worthy of perpetuation or not. There has also been an inundation of 'scissors-and-paste' books, 'case-books' as they are sometimes called, collecting what are often described as 'essential articles', either on an author, or very often on some single work. These are directed at undergraduates, who would be better employed in reading further novels by George Eliot than a number of articles on *Middlemarch*. They are obviously profitable to the publishers, who compete with each other in such series, so that for works that are in the fashion it is possible to find more than one such collection; in some cases they virtually duplicate each other. New literary periodicals have appeared, some excellent, others of very doubtful value, at a time when the importance and interest of the contributions to the older established journals have on the whole declined. There has been a proliferation of 'news-letters', a few covering a wide area, many devoted to minor figures. These report all that is being done, contain queries, and suggest 'research opportunities'. One serious result of this over-production is that it has become impossible to keep up with 'the literature of the subject' and many who give up trying to do so in despair may miss work that is of real value and importance.

We all know the reason for this over-production. It is the result of the over-importance given to publication in making and in renewing university appointments, and in giving promotion. The pressure to publish has always been strong in the universities of the United States. It is becoming increasingly strong in the universities of Great Britain. More and more graduate students want to work towards a doctorate, often cynically referred to as a 'union card'.[9] I am a great believer in a period of graduate study for the ablest of our students. I am not a great believer in the doctoral thesis as its necessary or even most worthwhile goal. There are some for whom it is obviously the right road: they know what they want to do, the kind of topic and the area they wish to work in, and what skills they must acquire. They need to be helped by older workers in their field, to whom they can bring their questions and problems and from whom they can learn the necessary skills and methods. But there are others of great ability and intelligence, who have not in this way discovered their course, who are forced to look round for a topic for a thesis that nobody else has worked on, or is working on, that comes to hang round their necks, like the Ancient Mariner's albatross, assuming an importance in their minds and lives altogether disproportionate to the value they derive from working on it. When, at last, they succeed in completing the thesis and 'satisfying the examiners', they have to start all over again to turn it into a readable book.

In 1973 Professor Gombrich contributed an article on 'Research in the Humanities: Ideals and Idols' to a number of *Daedalus*, the Journal of the American Academy of Arts and Sciences, devoted to 'The Search for Knowledge'.[10] Asserting that the activities covered by the term 'research' in the sciences and the arts differ fundamentally, he deplored the temptation in arts faculties to ape the sciences, which has resulted in the growth of an academic 'industry', that 'only rarely "advances the subject" and quite often impedes its growth'. In my inaugural lecture at Oxford in 1967 I said much the same:

A real deformation of values is suggested by the common use of such terms as 'productive scholars' and 'scholarly output' as if scholars should be assessed on the same basis as machines. I have even had it said to me that if there were no pressure to engage in original research and to publish university teachers would lapse into idleness. This is to equate scholarship with sewing mail-bags or picking oakum. Underlying the phrases used and this fear of idleness is a general failure of nerve in the universities: a feeling that they must justify themselves by pointing to tangible and measureable achievements, and that in them work, like justice, must not only be done but must be seen to be done. So many articles and so many books published by a department in so many years can be put in as evidence; so many hours of reading, and thinking, and of what all universities have more and more crowded out—'Blessed Idleness', the true seed-plot of thought—cannot be so weighed. Their effects on the academic community itself, and on the young people who pass through it into the world of affairs cannot be quantified.[11]

Professor Gombrich went on, following Bacon's lead, to list four classes of idols, which 'divert the humanities from their course'. First comes *idola quantitatis*, 'the belief that the recording of all available data must precede all other research', the search for 'completeness'. The second is *idola novitatis*, by which we 'prefer the new to the true'.[12] The third, related to the second, is *idola temporis*, the idols of the age: 'the lure of newly developed intellectual and mechanical tools which seem to promise prestige to those who "apply" them to the humanities'.[13] The fourth is *idola academica*: the distortion that comes from the dividing of the arts subjects into different 'disciplines' and 'departments', bringing about a 'timid territorialism', and beyond this, a bias created by teaching a syllabus that 'inevitably carries over into research' so that scholarship becomes geared to the teaching of a subject.

The distinction between research in the sciences and the arts is reflected in the fact that most scientists are able to complete their work and present their theses in the time given them, whereas most doctoral candidates in arts need extensions of time and many, even with generous extensions, do not finish at all. The scientist works on a well-defined problem, and whether his results are positive or negative he has 'advanced his subject', and can publish his results in the relevant journal. His fellow working on an arts subject has to acquire a body of knowledge relevant to his topic, which involves him in extensive reading. He may have to acquire new skills and learn about other subjects than those he worked on for his first degree; he may also have to acquire at least a reading knowledge of other languages, and possibly to travel to search for material in libraries here or abroad. Most of the time given him is spent in amassing material. The distinction can also be seen in the fact that many scientists, and most notably many mathematicians, do their most original and important work when they are comparatively young, whereas many scholars produce their most significant work in middle age, or even after retirement. The present trend towards demanding the completion of a long, exhaustive doctoral thesis as the most important qualification for admission to the profession of a university teacher demands too much and too little of many graduates in the humanities: too much because it is expecting of them a precocious maturity, too little because it only too often focuses their interests too narrowly, and depresses their genial spirits. I am sure that any period of graduate study ought to include a piece of investigation, but it should be on a well-defined subject. If the subject appears to be expanding beyond the limits of what can be handled in a short thesis, it should be redefined. I am not saying that we should not cherish and insist upon support for those who have discovered their bent early and are ready to take on a large subject and to work on it in depth; but there are others for whom a wider range of study with a short thesis, done as an exercise in method, would be a far better preparation for teaching in a university and might well lead to more valuable and original work in later life. I take great pride in those scholars who worked with me and successfully completed doctoral theses which they later published; but I am also proud of those who were content with a B.Litt.,[14] which may or may not have resulted in an article or have developed into a book, and have since established themselves as teachers and scholars.

The stress on publication as a condition of gaining tenure or promotion is not, I think, unconnected with a certain lack of interest in literary studies in the world outside the universities. We have been much less successful than some of our colleagues in the humanities in disseminating knowledge and appreciation of the results of our studies. Historians, as well as engaging in severely professional research, write books that are respected by their colleagues and are also widely read. They are to be found on the bookshelves of persons who are not professional historians. The musicologists, the archaeologists, and the art-historians have been similarly successful. They have been able to make use of the radio and of recordings, and the archaeologists and art-historians have had television also, in addition to publication in book form. Musicologists have been able to arouse a lively interest in what might have seemed recondite music, played on original instruments, and stripped of later improvements. Why are people willing to tolerate hearing well-loved works such as Handel's *Messiah* in its original form, but cannot be expected to bear productions of Shakespeare without adventitious adornments and interpretations? The two subjects that appear to have retreated into the world of academe are the two that once would have been regarded as of central concern to all educated men and women: philosophy and literature. I do not share the gloomy view that people are not reading widely for themselves today. I see on the bookshelves of unacademic friends volumes of poetry and novels, and can point to the huge sales of Penguin classics, and of similar books published by others, who have followed that great benefactor of the human race, Sir Allen Lane, into the paper-back market. I do not see works of literary criticism or literary scholarship on the shelves of those not professionally concerned, although I do see a good many literary biographies. I connect this partly with the overvaluing of publication as against teaching in the universities, which has made what we can do to, or make of, literature more important than disseminating the understanding and enjoyment of what great works of the imagination can give.

Looking back over my life, I am deeply grateful that I was never under any pressure to publish. I also think that, as it turned out, I was lucky in that the modern system of graduate awards did not exist in my day. I doubt whether I should have had the nerve to give up two further years at Oxford, with possible extensions of time, for a temporary post of one term at Birmingham. But I also doubt whether, if I had refused this opportunity, I should, in a period of acute shortage of posts, have found employment in a university. I think I was right to feel that I was not ready to work on writers of the stature of Shakespeare and Donne without much more knowledge than I had. Although I came to realize that I had taken a wrong course, taking it had taught me a variety of skills that I was very glad to have acquired, and had given me a background of reading and thinking that became highly relevant later on. If I had been able to stay on at Oxford, with extensions of time, to submit work on *The Scale of Perfection* for a doctorate, and had then felt obliged to proceed with an edition, what I now see as a misjudgement that bore fruit years later would have become a fatal mistake. Of course, I am conscious of failures, errors, and follies, but I have only one great regret. I share with Sir Andrew Aguecheek the wish that I had been able to bestow more of my time 'in the tongues'. I wish it had been possible for me to have spent another year at school, so that I could have been competent to read Honour Moderations in Classics at Oxford before reading English. Apart from this, I feel that I have done what I was meant to do. I have been greatly fortunate to have been able to spend my life in the company of my betters: poets, dramatists, novelists, makers of imagined worlds of all kinds, creators of profoundly significant images of human life and experience, and to find in their works and to help others to find

> Knowledge and increase of enduring joy
> From the great Nature that exists in works
> Of mighty Poets.[15]

I am glad to end with a quotation from Wordsworth, for like him, *sed longo intervallo*, I would wish to be considered as a teacher or as nothing.

NOTES

1   *English Renaissance Studies*, edited by John Carey (Oxford, 1980).
2   I was a beneficiary of the Fisher Education Act of 1918, by which local authorities gave free places at secondary schools to able children at the age of eleven, renewable on the results of the School Certificate Examination for two further years at sixteen, and by County Major Scholarships to any who won awards at Oxford or Cambridge. I was fortunate in being under the London County Council, an enlightened and generous authority.
3   The phrase is Milton's, attacking 'those that pretend to be great Rabbies' but 'have bin but Ferrets and Moushunts [Weasels] of an Index' (*Of Reformation*).

4 This policy has borne fruit in Eric Dobson's brilliant and fascinating study, *The Origins of 'Ancrene Wisse'* (Oxford, 1976). Even those who cannot accept his bold attempt to give a name to the author, must delight in his lucid and authoritative handling of a mass of varied information on this tantalizing and delightful text.

5 I may, perhaps, be excused for my failure to continue working on *The Scale of Perfection* by the fact that it is still unedited. I gave my material to a former pupil, who worked on the text of Book I under Dorothy Everett for a B.Litt. She married and went out to Africa. Her work was handed on to another scholar, who has died; but she is now back in England and assisting yet another scholar to complete an edition of Book I, which I am glad to say is about to go to press. I gave my material on Book II to another scholar but have no news of his progress.

6 Some people to whom I have repeated this remark have taken it as offensive. I took it as a high compliment and as a characteristic response to my own remark, which some might have thought impertinent.

7 Our task was to make recommendations covering the whole untidy system—or lack of system—of higher education, although people often speak as if the Robbins Committee was only concerned with the universities.

8 In saying this, I am thinking of the average standard of intelligence. I do not think the standard at the top has risen, and first classes are now, I think, more generously given than they were in my day. I think the alteration in the system of public examinations has led to undergraduates being, in some ways, less well prepared for work at the university than they were. The old School Certificate and Higher School Certificate required passes in certain groups of subjects, as did the old university entrance requirements. A disturbing development, which we did not anticipate when we reported in 1963, has been a marked swing against science in the schools and a consequent difficulty in filling the science places provided. A main beneficiary of this has been sociology. I do not know what the standard is there; but I rather doubt whether sociology makes a good undergraduate course.

9 Some who use this phrase seem to think it means entitlement to a post, but I fear it is more and more meaning only a 'closed shop'.

10 *Daedalus*, Spring 1973, reprinted in *Ideals and Idols* (London, 1979), 112–22.

11 *Literary Studies*, An Inaugural Lecture delivered before the University of Oxford on 1 June 1967 (Oxford, 1967).

12 'It is easy to propose a fresh reading if we treat a text cavalierly and disregard the intentions of the creator. . . . Unfortunately, such is the fabric of the academic industry that even an absurd reading will be accorded immortality in the footnotes.' (p. 117.)

13 'Vulnerability to intellectual fashions is the most depressing effect of the pressures created by the academic industry. Here, too, the cult can be particularly harmful to the young, who are easily impressed by a fresh and prestigious jargon.' (p. 118.)

14   The B.Litt. was established in 1895; the D.Phil. in 1917 under pressure to make Oxford compete with the attractive power of Germanic universities with their prestigious Ph.D. Both are degrees by thesis alone. The B.Phil., which began among the philosophers, is a degree by examination, with the option of substituting a short thesis for one of the papers. It has now spread to other Arts Faculties. Both the B.Litt. and the B.Phil. are now renamed as M.Litt. and M.Phil. to make clear they are not first degrees.

15   *The Prelude*, V, 593–5.

Appendix:

Literary Biography

The Presidential Address of the Modern Humanities Research Association read at University College, London, on 4 January 1980

'It is in the second half of our century that Biography has come of age, in this country at least,' said Robert Gittings in a lecture given in February 1976 to the Royal Society of Literature, published in *Essays by Divers Hands*, edited by Vincent Cronin (1979). He referred to a statement made a few years before in which it had been announced that 'the number of biographies published in this country had for the first time topped the thousand mark', and appealed to the experience of librarians, who find increasingly that stock and borrowing of non-fiction have increased and are increasing, and to the confirmation of this that a visit to any public library will provide, where biographies occupy a great deal of space and are shelved together irrespective of whether the subject is a monarch, or a politician, or a soldier, or a bishop, or a writer. Dr Gittings gave his lecture the title 'Artist upon Oath', using a phrase of Desmond MacCarthy's which differentiates the biographer from the creator of fictions, the poet or 'maker', whose creations must also face a test of truth, but not of truth of fact. A year later Dr Gittings delivered three lectures on 'The Art and Science of Biography' in Seattle, which he published in 1978 under the title *The Nature of Biography*. Here he made very large claims for the art he practises. In his preface he tells us that biography with him arose out of his attempts at poetry and declares that he still sees a relationship between the two arts, giving as his attempt at a phrase which would define the nature of biography that it is 'poetry with a conscience'. He tells us that he published in 1950 a book of verse, 'whose title-poem, *Wentworth Place*, was a series of impressions in verse of the two years spent by the poet Keats in the Hampstead house of that name':

This sequence, each part headed by an extract from Keats's letters, and often using adapted phrases from the same source, tried to reconstruct imaginatively his life during this period, when all his greatest poems were written. Like all poetry, it did not pretend to be a literal interpretation but rather a symbolic one; yet the symbols I used were the facts of his life. When this was printed, some stirrings of artistic conscience, or perhaps my previous training as an historian, made me question my own right to present Keats's life in this way, without having ascertained the truth on which my poetic assumptions were based. Did the Keats I had conceived ever exist? Out of that question arose my subsequent involvement in the writing of biography, and the attempt to find convincing outward warrant for the inner events of life, particularly the life of a creative artist such as Keats, and later, Hardy.

If 'poetry with a conscience' is a definition of biography, does Dr Gittings intend to imply that poets and novelists write without consciences? And was the conscience that made him question his right to make a poem out of his reading of the letters and poems that Keats wrote in his two years at Hampstead 'an artistic conscience'? He was not troubled by the question of whether he had given truthful expression to the impression made on him by his reading of the poems and letters that Keats wrote in those two wonderful years, but by a question that implicitly denies the right of the poet to create, using, modifying, or disregarding facts, his own image of truth. Should we blame Shelley for not enquiring more deeply into the facts of Keats's life and death before writing *Adonais*, and do we value the poem any the less because we know that Keats was not, in fact, 'snuffed out by an article'? What Dr Gittings seems to be evading by his definition is the obvious fact that however much the modern biographer *may* employ the techniques of the poet or the novelist, he *must* employ the skills of the historian, and his conscience must be the conscience of a historian, whether or not he has in addition the conscience of a poet. When Dr Gittings describes his involvement in the writing of biography as 'the attempt to find convincing outward warrant for the inner events of life, particularly the life of a creative artist such as Keats, and, later, Hardy', he begs a very large question: whether the inner events of a life can ever in any proper sense be known as we can know dates of birth and publication. And does he by speaking of 'convincing outward warrant' intend the implication that what they did and where they went, and what friends or acquaintances or enemies said of them is more convincing warrant for the inner lives of writers such as Keats and Hardy than what they wrote?

At the close of his last lecture, Dr Gittings sums up by saying that biography is no longer viewed as a kind of poor relation to either literature or history (although he argues for its importance to the historian and the literary critic), and ends by expressing his faith as a biographer who assumes that 'all life has something worth recording, and recording truly for all time', and that 'the truth about men and women is totally desirable, helpful, and important'. He believes that 'biography, and the exploration of human life, in all its strength and frailty, will continue to grow, beyond its relatively short past history, to one of the leading features of the creative output of future generations'.

As a devoted reader of biographies of all kinds, I have no wish to undervalue in any way the skill, devotion, and artistry required to produce a good biography, or the enjoyment it gives; and I do not doubt that Dr Gittings is right in believing that biographies, good, bad, and indifferent, will continue to pour from the presses in the future. What I cannot accept is the elevation of biography to the status which has always been accorded to the works of those 'peerless poets' who range freely 'within the zodiac of their own wits', or, who, out of their experience, fashion tales of imagination, such as dramatists, poets, and novelists: 'creative artists'. Dr Gittings rightly applied the term 'creative artists' to Keats and Hardy in his introduction, presumably to distinguish them from other literary artists. I cannot accept that the same adjective should be applied to their biographers, however much they may employ the novelist's art of arrangement, suggestion, and the dramatic highlighting of events.

In 1927 Virginia Woolf, in an article on 'The New Biography', reprinted in *Granite and Rainbow* (1958), declared that the author's relation to his subject had changed: 'Whether friend or enemy, admiring or critical, he is an equal. . . . Moreover, he does not think himself constrained to follow every step of the way. Raised upon a little eminence which his independence has made for him, he sees his subject spread about him. He chooses; he synthesizes; in short, he has ceased to be the chronicler; he has become an artist.' Twelve years later she returned to the subject of biography in an essay on 'The Art of Biography', reprinted in *The Death of the Moth* (1942), in which she began by asking the question 'Is biography an art?'; and came to the conclusion that the biographer is 'a craftsman, not an artist; and his work is not a work of art but something betwixt and between'. For biography, she wrote, 'imposes conditions, and those conditions are that it must be based on fact. And by fact in biography we mean facts that can be verified by other people besides the artist. If he invents facts as an artist invents them—facts that no one else can verify— and tries to combine them with facts of the other sort, they destroy each other.' She illustrated her distinction from the works of her friend Lytton Strachey, a writer, who, she said, 'wished to write poetry or plays but was doubtful of his creative power'. Biography offered him an alternative, since by 1918 'it was possible to tell the truth about the dead. . . . To recreate them, to show them as they really were, was a task that called for gifts analogous to the poet's or the novelist's, yet did not ask that inventive power in which he found himself lacking.' Passing by *Eminent Victorians*, as 'short studies with something of the over-emphasis and the foreshortening of caricatures', she praised *Queen Victoria*, since there Strachey had treated biography as a craft, but stigmatized *Elizabeth and Essex* as a failure in which fact and fiction had 'refused to mix'.

I would not (with Virginia Woolf) deny the title of artist to a skilled and sensitive biographer, for 'artist' is a wide term, and I am happy to regard biography as an important and interesting form of literature, which is also a wide term. It can include sermons, philosophical treatises, political pamphlets, histories, and literary criticism, all of which can display a high degree of literary skill and literary artistry as well as calling for the exercise of the imagination. All these are non-autonomous literary forms to which we have to apply standards that are other than literary. A sermon must edify, for that is the purpose of preaching, and a sermon that does not edify is a poor sermon, however great the rhetorical art of the preacher; a philosophic treatise must satisfy the standards of logical rigour, and obey the laws that govern rational discourse; a historical work must provide us with information that is verifiable, and give a true record of events as well as an interpretation of them. Biography takes its place among these non-autonomous literary forms, and not with poetry in its various forms, dramatic, narrative, or lyrical; for poetry, although it may edify, or appeal to verifiable fact, or include rational arguments, need not do so. It has to stand one test only: of imaginative truth and imaginative consistency.

To make distinctions and to insist on any kind of hierarchy is unpopular today, and to stress the importance of *poiēsis*, imaginative creation, over other literary forms, is to row against fashionable currents. Claims similar to those made by Dr Gittings for biography are also being made, with great force and intellectual energy, for literary criticism. Particularly in America, but to some extent in this country too, the methods of *la nouvelle critique* as it has developed in France have been adopted. By this, imaginative literature is treated as only one mode of discourse among others, and denied any privileged status ·as having a special value, providing us with unique insights into the nature of reality and of human experience, beyond what we derive from history or philosophical discourse. Criticism, it is declared, has a function beyond the obviously academic and pedagogical. It has, that is to say, not merely a service function: to increase our understanding and enjoyment of works of art. It is 'part of the world of letters, and has its own mixed philosophical and literary, reflective and figural strength'. 'Deconstruction, as it has come to be called, refuses to identify the force of literature with any concept of embodied meaning and shows how deeply such logocentric or incarnationist perspectives have influenced the way we think about art.' It asserts the primacy of language over meaning, and the critic, presented with words whose meaning is indeterminate, becomes a creator among the play of significances the words of the text emit. I have been quoting from Professor Geoffrey Hartman's introduction to *Deconstruction and Criticism*, a collection of essays just published by five members of the Faculty of Arts at Yale. A slightly different emphasis was given by Professor Hillis Miller, one of the contributors, in an admirably lucid account of the critics of the Geneva School in *The Critical Quarterly* in 1966. For them, he wrote, criticism is 'primordially consciousness of the consciousness of another, the transposition of the mental universe of an author into the interior space of the critic's mind'. They are, therefore, not interested in the external form of individual works, and often prefer to use incomplete works, or drafts, which 'may allow better access to the intimate tone or quality of a mind than a perfected masterpiece'. Their concern is with the subjective structure of the mind revealed by the whole body of an author's writings. This sounds like a digression; but it has, I think, relevance to my subject, which is literary biography and not biography in general. Deconstruction in its pure form rejects the historical. All works of all times are only what a modern reader can make of them; he reads meanings, or imports meanings, into texts. The Geneva School is not interested in perfected works of art but uses them to attempt to arrive at the consciousness out of which they sprang. They are a means by which 'a subjectivity enters a subjectivity'. The two schools are alike in their indifference to the works that the author made: the one declaring their meaning to be irrecoverable, the other that their value lies not in themselves but in what they reveal to us of the writer's inner life. The literary biographer is at first sight opposed to both schools. Biography is rooted in history; the biographer is committed to truth of fact and to a truthful record of events in his subject's life. But the most important events in the life of a writer are his creations of works of art. They are the *raison d'être* for writing his life. Who would bother to write the life of a young man who began his career as a medical student, gave up the medical profession for the profession of a writer, and died of tuberculosis at the age of twenty-six, if the literary works he produced in his short life were of no value? His life might be a subject for a pathetic novel but hardly for a biography; and the novel would hardly in its dimensions rival *War and Peace* as biographies of Keats tend to do. Yet I have recently begun to feel that the art of the modern literary biographer, which aims at presenting the real man, either by finding, as Dr Gittings put it, 'convincing outward warrant for the inner events of his life', or, as Professor Edel has put it, by leading us 'from the work to the man, from the mask to the face and to the mind and consciousness', shows something of the same devaluing of the creating and shaping spirit of imagination of great writers that I feel in the followers of *la nouvelle critique*.

The literary biographer has to accept that he is regarded with even more dislike and distaste than the critic by poets and novelists, who dread becoming the object of his enquiries. While they may regard their critics with something of contempt, as blinkered, obtuse, and unfair, they regard with fear and loathing the idea that, after death, unprotected by the law of libel, or the decencies that inhibit us from reading letters not addressed to ourselves, or snooping round the house of another person when he is out, they will be the prey of a biographer who, with the zeal of a detective and the nose of a bloodhound, will enter every sanctum of their private lives in search of the 'real man'.

> While I live the Owls
> When I die the Ghouls!!!

wrote Tennyson by the side of an epigram on the poet's fate by Thomas Hood. From Wordsworth and Coleridge to Eliot and Auden the same note is struck. Eliot, as we all know, in a memorandum added to his will, instructed his wife to give no assistance to any biographer. Whether this was to protect himself or his wife I do not know. I suspect both motives operated. Auden asked his friends to destroy any of his letters to them that were in their possession. In the prefaces and reviews of Auden which are collected under the title *Forewords and Afterwords*, he recurs to the subject again and again:

If the Muses could lobby for their interest, all biographical research into the lives of artists would probably be prohibited by law, and historians of the individual would have to confine themselves to those who act but do not make—generals, criminals, eccentrics, courtesans and the like, about whom information is not only more interesting but less misleading. Good artists—the artist *manqué* is another matter— never make satisfactory heroes for novelists because their life stories, even when interesting for themselves, are peripheral and less significant than their productions.

This was from a preface to a selection from Edgar Allan Poe, written in 1950. Fourteen years later, in an introduction to the Signet edition of Shakespeare's *Sonnets*, he returned to the charge, combating the idea that if we could establish beyond doubt the identity of the Friend, the Dark Lady, the Rival Poet, this would in any way illuminate our understanding of the sonnets themselves. This notion, he wrote,

seems to me to betray, either a complete misunderstanding of the nature of the relation between art and life or an attempt to rationalize and justify plain vulgar idle curiosity. . . . Idle curiosity is an ineradicable vice of the human mind. All of us like to discover the secrets of our neighbours, particularly the ugly ones. This has always been so, and, probably, always will be. What is relatively new, however . . . is a blurring of the borderline between desire for truth and idle curiosity, until today it has been so thoroughly erased that we can indulge in the latter without the slightest pang of conscience. A great deal of what today passes for scholarly research is an activity no different from reading somebody's correspondence when he is out of the room, and it doesn't make it morally any better if he is out of the room because he is in his grave.

He went on to add that the relation between a poet's life and his works is 'at the same time too self-evident to require comment— every work of art is, in one sense, a self-disclosure—and too complicated ever to unravel. . . . Further, it should be borne in mind that most genuine artists would prefer that no biography should be written.'

Both Professor Edel and Dr Gittings have written of the lengths their subjects went to in order to frustrate their bio-graphers. In *Literary Biography* (1959, reprinted 1973), lectures given at Toronto in 1936 when he had published only the first volume of his massive *Life of Henry James*, Edel writes that James offers us 'the unique picture of a novelist who, in the most premeditated fashion in the world, arranged a tug of war between himself and his future biographer'. First his letters: 'Sometimes', Edel writes, 'he wrote full warm letters largely about his art. He wrote gossipy letters as well, but he seldom talked about himself. . . . Concerning himself, the details are always general and often trivial: the intimate glimpses are few and rather guarded. His letters are remarkable for their fluency, their cordi-ality, their vitality; they are the overflow of a man's creativity, the surplus of his genius. They are often highly descriptive and they are nearly always filled with fine free phrases thrown off with the greatest of liberality.' At the time he wrote this, Edel tells us, he had read 'some ten thousand' letters by James, and he added as his general comment that 'in this biographical abun-dance much more is concealed than is revealed. The letters are a part of the novelist's work, of his literary self, a part of his capacity for playing out personal relations as a great game of life ... we seem indeed to watch him as he watches himself in a mirror.' (pp. 34–6.) Nearly twenty years later, when the number of letters he had read had amounted to fifteen thousand, in the introduction to the first volume of his edition of the *Letters* (1974), Edel came to the same conclusion. The letters of James, he declared, 'belong ... to literature and also to literary psychology'. Although he writes that they 'constitute one of the greatest self-portraits in all literature', the reader 'must deduce the integral James from his personal documents and the anecdotes or memories of others' (p. xv).

Edel reported that James often enjoined his correspondents 'burn this, please, burn, burn', the letters surviving with their disregarded injunction. Before he had completed his first novel James had written that 'Artists as time goes on will be likely to take the alarm, empty their table drawers and level the approaches to their privacy. The critics, psychologists and gossip-mongers may then glean amid the stubble.' Three years later he wrote that there should be a 'certain sanctity in all appeals to the generosity and forbearance of posterity, and that a man's table drawers and pockets should not be turned inside out'. James, Edel tell us, had a secret drawer in his desk; but when it was discovered and opened it was found to contain only a gout remedy and a prescription for eyeglasses. Later in life, when at the turn of the century he was concerned about his health, he made a huge bonfire in his garden at Lamb House and burned the correspondence of years. Edel comments that James 'would have exclaimed with Dickens who lit a similar blaze at Gad's Hill: "would to God every letter I have ever written were on that pile"' (pp. 37–8). Two years before his death he sent instructions to his nephew, his literary executor, declaring his 'utter and absolute abhorrence of any attempted biography or the giving to the world by "the family" or by any person for whom my approval has any sanctity, of any part or parts of my private correspondence' (*Letters*, p. xvi). In a small masterpiece, *The Aspern Papers*, and in two of his supernatural tales, *The Real Right Thing* and *Sir Dominick Ferrand*, he gave fictitious expression to this same 'utter and absolute abhorrence'. The 'real right thing' is to leave the lives of authors alone and read their works, and Miss Tita does 'the great thing' when she destroys the letters the poet Jeffrey Aspern had written to her aunt.

James wrote and published some autobiographical works. Hardy went much further. Both *The Early Life of Thomas Hardy* and *The Later Years of Thomas Hardy* (with the exception of its final chapters) were not in fact biographies. Although they were published with his widow's name on the title-pages, they were Hardy's own autobiography, written in the third person. Hardy's own manuscripts, from which his wife made typescripts, were destroyed, as were the bulk of the letters and diaries and notebooks from which Hardy worked. Professor Purdy, who elucidated the matter, describes *The Early Life* as 'immensely valuable as a personal and intimate document', but adds 'it has naturally many significant silences and some characters in the story are not mentioned at all. . . . The conditions of Hardy's birth and childhood are idealized. The bitterness of his struggle for an education and a profession and the suffering of his first marriage find no reflection. . . . This is only to say that Hardy set down what he chose, free from the obligations of formal biography. The measure of detachment he achieved is remarkable.' Professor Purdy worked at his bibliographical study of Hardy with the 'approval and generous support of Mrs Hardy and Sir Sidney Cockerell, Hardy's literary executors', and his book was dedicated to Mrs Hardy 'in affectionate remembrance'. In stating that Mrs Hardy 'loyally preserved the fiction of her authorship to the end', he refers to the fiction as 'this innocent deception'. Dr Gittings takes a much severer view of the matter.

Why is it that authors are so strongly opposed to the idea of becoming the subjects of a biography? We do not hear the same protests from statesmen and politicians, from generals or admirals, judges or bishops, from scientists or from other artists: painters, sculptors, musicians, actors, or actresses. They seem to view with at least equanimity, and some even with complacency, the prospect of their lives being investigated and presented to the world. I do not believe that it is because the lives of authors contain more ugly secrets than the lives of their fellow men. One reason, I think, is that, as Auden wrote, the lives of most authors—there are of course exceptions—are not usually very interesting or exciting to relate. They are rarely involved in public affairs or exciting events or adventures. Biographers of public figures must necessarily spend much of their time and space on public affairs, and although a politician's private life may assist (or sometimes disastrously affect) his career, the focus of the biographer must be on the part his subject played in public affairs and much of his work must be given over to explaining the political situation in which his subject operated. No modern biographer of Lloyd George could fail to mention today the activities that earned him the nickname of 'the Goat', any more than a biographer of Parnell could at any time have avoided his relation with Mrs O'Shea and her husband, although today the matter could be handled more freely than it could have been in the early years of this century. But the connections between a statesman's policies, his skill in advancing them, his judgements or misjudgements of the political, economic, or international situation, and his private life are not of great importance. Although the biographer may give us a vivid impression of his personality, this, even if it is disagreeable, does not greatly affect our judgement of his achievement. The writer, on the other hand, knows that the focus of his biographer will be almost wholly on his personal and private life, and that the investigation of this may reveal not only what he himself would prefer to keep secret; it may also painfully involve the lives of others, his family and friends, whose personal misfortunes, sorrows, or defects will also come to light. The amount of gossip, anecdote, and trivial information available to the industrious biographer of any recently dead writer is today almost unlimited. Nobody now destroys letters, however intimate, since their value has soared in the sale-rooms, and few who knew him, however slightly, are unwilling to talk. What the writer fears is that attention will be directed away from his achievement to the circumstances, events, and pains and griefs of his life, and that the search for the 'real man' will blunt and distort response to that 'second self' who wrote the poems or novels and 'lives and speaks' through them. I have taken the term 'second self' from Edward Dowden, who used it in speaking of George Eliot. He was quoted by Professor Kathleen Tillotson in her inaugural lecture in 1959, *The Tale and the Teller*. In speaking of George Eliot's 'second self' Dowden meant 'the form that most persists in the mind after reading her novels'. 'The second self', he wrote, 'is more substantial than any mere human personality' and has 'fewer reserves'; while 'behind it, lurks well pleased the veritable historical self secure from impertinent observation and criticism'. It is this 'second self' by which the writer wishes to live. His fear is that the works he has created will be read for clues to the 'real man' behind the work; will be interpreted by the conception the biographer has arrived at of his 'life-myth'; or will be impoverished either by being treated as a form of therapy through which he worked out his neuroses, or by being tied to events and situations in which they may have partially originated but which do not account for what they are; or will be distorted by being treated as dishonestly disguising some real truth which the biographer has ferreted out. In 1971, in *The Burden of the Past and the English Poet*, Professor Bate pleaded for a 'step-by-step biography of the drama of each writer's life . . . a more sympathetic—a more psychologically informed—use of biography: a recognition of what the artist confronted in what were for him the most important things with which to struggle (his craft and his whole relation with tradition, with what has been done and with what he hopes can still be done)'. Professor Bate's own practice, as exemplified by his distinguished life of Keats in 1963, shows that he did not intend by his plea that a biographer should neglect the duty of informing us accurately of the circumstances and events of his subject's life. He does not hold with Professor Northrop Frye that 'Poetry can only be made out of other poems, novels out of other novels'; or, with Professor Harold Bloom's view, which might be described in racing terms as 'By Bate out of Frye': that the poet is solely engaged in an interior struggle with his precursors. But Professor Bate's ideal seems to me, except in rare cases, to be simply beyond human powers. His own life of Keats reaches to some seven hundred pages, and Keats died young, his life as a writer spanning barely six years. Edel's life of Henry James occupies close on seventeen hundred pages. It is impossible to compute how long it would have been if, in addition to all it tells us about James's family and friends, his travels, his habits of work, his various abodes, it had treated the novels in the manner in which Professor Bate is able to handle Keats's development as a poet, had dealt with James's absorption and transformation of the traditions of the American, English, French, and Russian novel, not to mention the traditions of the short story. There must surely be some division of labour here between the biographer and the literary critic, and each must recognize that neither of them can reach to more than partial truth about the man, or about his work, or about the relation between them.

As a critic I have always recognized the importance of biographical information, since I hold that a poem or a novel is a historical object produced by a human being at a certain time in certain circumstances. Although it is autonomous in the important sense that it has an existence independent of the experiences and emotions that the writer drew on to make it, yet experiences and emotions are among the causes that have gone to its making, as well as observations of the world of nature and the world of human actions, and the literary traditions the writer could draw upon. It can in some measure be understood and enjoyed without all this knowledge, but knowledge of all kinds can assist both understanding and enjoyment. This is the humanist approach which is committed to what Professor Hartman calls 'logocentric and incarnationist perspectives' and to the essential temporality of human experience and human artefacts.

This said, it seems the height of ingratitude that I should make any complaint against Professor Edel, when I recall the enormous pleasure and profit I have received from his *Life of Henry James*, apart altogether from what I owe to him for his labours in editing the *Complete Tales*, and the (alas, I fear, forever suspended) Bodley Head edition of the novels. And, as if this were not enough for one man to have done, he is now at work upon, not a complete edition of the fifteen thousand letters, but a comprehensive selection. I greatly welcome his decision here as it looks as if this will be an edition most of us will be able to afford to buy. No doubt, when the edition is completed, he will supply in some form a check-list of letters omitted, with the locations. I have nothing but admiration for the manner in which Edel organized the mass of material he had to handle, and I applaud his bold decision to avoid a strictly chronological for a partially thematic treatment. This alone would justify him in regarding himself as an artist in biography. At times I became a little uncertain of the year I was in, and I must own I should have liked rather more detailed references than he provided in the original five-volume edition. In the revised two-volume edition for Penguin Books in 1977, to which as the 'definitive edition' I shall be referring, all references were omitted in the interests of economy.

My one complaint is about Edel's treatment of James's fictions, which are relentlessly tied to the 'life-myth' which gives the biographer his story, or else are interpreted as expressions of the personal emotions of the period at which they were written. We are constantly taken back to Quincy Street, to the dominating mother, and the weak, compliant, limping father, stumping about the house with his wooden leg, to Aunt Kate, to Henry's sibling rivalry with William, his elder brother, and to his 'uncertainty about the trustworthiness of women', his shrinking from real experience, and his choice of celibacy. This continually deprives the works of their complexity and variety, and reduces the characters, particularly James's wonderful gallery of portraits of ladies, to a few unconvincing stereotypes. Thus Christina Light, as she appears in *Roderick Hudson*, is typed as a 'struggling, questioning fated female', and we are told that 'in later transformations she will become Madame Merle and Kate Croy' (i. 414). Her transformation from the Christina we meet as an unmarried young woman in Rome to the Princess Casamassima, dabbling in radical politics, whom we meet in Hyacinth Robinson's London is wholly convincing; but I cannot recognize her in either Madame Merle or Kate Croy. Even stranger is Edel's discovery of the Quincy Street household behind the characters in poor Hyacinth's story. James wrote *The Bostonians* and *The Princess Casamassima* in London when he had settled there after the death of his mother and his father and the consequent loss of the family home in Boston. Both, like their successor, *The Tragic Muse*, are long novels and show less mastery of form than *Portrait of a Lady*, the culmination of James's early period. Edel does not ascribe this to the fact that James was attempting a different kind of novel, with a wider scope, handling social and political themes. *The Bostonians*, we are told, 'was the novel in which James wrote out the immediate anguish of the collapse of his old American ties, and he coupled this with a kind of vibrating anger that Boston should be so unfriendly as to let him go' (i. 744); and in *The Princess Casamassima*, 'a novel which seemed farthest removed from himself, James wrote out the personal emotions of this period. . . . He re-imagined his subterranean world of feeling in terms of his hero's revolt, despair and need for action. He siphoned off into his work a lugubrious state of mind, leaving himself freer and more possessed of his mature self.' (i. 780–1.) As for the persons of the novel, in Paul Muniment 'there is a touch of Wiliam James' since the portrait of Hyacinth and Paul is 'James's characteristic picture of the younger man who feels misunderstood by the older, to whom he is nevertheless deeply attached'; and Paul's sister, Rosy, 'who like Alice James is bed-ridden', has 'asperities and hostilities' that 'portray not a little of that unpleasant side of Alice' (i. 777). James's sense of

being bereft of his parents is emphasized by the number of fathers and mothers Henry allots to Hyacinth. There had been Hyacinth's original parents, Lord Frederick Purvis, murdered by his French mother, Florentine Vivier, whom he had seen but once in the Millbank infirmary. There is Mr Vetch, the old violinist, and the dressmaker Miss Pynsent who brought up the boy; both constitute a parental pair, advising, admonishing, helping. . . . And then he has acquired still another, a disciplined and resolute father, in the person of the anarchist Dietrich Hoffendahl, seen in a nocturnal interview, to whom the bookbinder had pledged absolute obedience. Hoffendahl in James's imagination belongs with the crippled elder Henry James—for Henry endows the anarchist with a maimed arm. (i. 780.)

Actually, Hoffendahl's hand had been mutilated during the tortures he had suffered while imprisoned, when he had heroically refused to name his associates. It is the thought of this 'mutilated hand' that fires the imagination of Hyacinth, who, when he hears that the hero is actually in London 'was in a state of inward exaltation, possessed by an intense desire to stand face to face with the sublime Hoffendahl, to hear his voice and touch his mutilated hand'. For here is a martyr, a man who has suffered and not merely endlessly talked. We seem a very long way from the easy, compliant father we have been told of, stumping about the house with his wooden leg. But the ways of the imagination are strange, so strange that it is perhaps better not to try to map them. *The Princess Casamassima* is James's most Dickensian novel, a great London novel. He told us that Hyacinth 'sprang up' for him 'out of the London pavement'. Hyacinth's origins have affinities with the melodramatic element in so many of Dickens's plots, while Rosy Muniment has always reminded me of sharp little Jenny Wren, who like her, to their authors' credit, does not bear her infirmities with saintly meekness.

In dealing with the stories, Professor Edel's summaries at times deform the story, or obscure its point, or neglect its literary origins, in order to make it reveal James's psychological make-up. Thus, some of the earliest tales are said to show a preoccupation with the mystery of womankind. Among these Edel puts 'A Landscape Painter', which is an entertaining remaking of Tennyson's 'The Lord of Burleigh', in which the village maiden, whom the wealthy lord had wooed disguised as a poor landscape painter, pines and dies 'With the burden of an honour/Unto which she was not born'. In James's story a rich man has broken off his engagement on discovering that his fiancée is mercenary. He goes off to a seaside cottage to paint, lodging with an old sea-captain and his daughter. He woos her and, thinking that she loves him for himself, marries her. But she had looked at his diary and knew all along that he was a wealthy man and tells him so after marriage. 'It was the act of a false woman', he exclaims. But she only smiles at him, for after all, if she had deceived him he had deceived her. 'Osborne's Revenge' has some connection with Browning's poem 'A Light Woman'. Osborne has been told that his dearly loved friend's suicide was on account of his being jilted by a girl, and he decides to revenge his friend by making the girl fall in love with him and then jilting her. When he meets her he finds her to be charming, intelligent, and reserved, quite the reverse of a coquette. In the end he learns the truth. She had never jilted his friend. She was all the time engaged to the other man, was much distressed by the friend's persecution of her, and had never heard of his suicide. Having told the story, Edel comments:

Thus a woman who seemed a flirt and a vampire turns out to be noble and virtuous and innocent of all the designs attributed to her by the vengeful hero. The tale is that of a man seeking to understand a woman and discovering that he has been in error from start to finish. It speaks of a serious doubt: what if Henry's reading of women were wrong? He was aware, as this tale reveals, of the disparity between appearance and reality; and in its primitive fashion it is, therefore, a forerunner of future tales of bewilderment. It is also a story of a man's chronic difficulty with the opposite sex. (i. 215.)

But the girl was in reality just what she appeared to be, good, charming, and modest. She never seemed a flirt or a vampire. It was only the spiteful gossip of a jealous woman that represented her as a flirt and a jilt. These are trivial stories, prentice work; but on occasion the subtlety and ambiguity of an impressive story is destroyed, as when the unhappy Mrs Ambient in 'The Author of Beltraffio' is described as 'the baleful female of many of James's tales', and more than once compared in her 'ferocity' to Medea. Edel's summary of the story agrees with the *Notebooks*, but disregards how much the tale James wrote differs from his scheme there, which he thought required 'prodigious delicacy of touch; and even then *is* probably too gruesome'. It ignores the addition of the sinister Miss Ambient, her brother's disciple, and the obtuse act of the narrator, Ambient's young admirer, who tries to convert Mrs Ambient from the horror she feels at her husband's work by giving her proof-sheets of his new book to read while she is sitting up with her sick child. The malevolent sister-in-law gives her explanation of what happened in the locked bedroom that night, why the doctor was sent away, and the medicines not given. The narrator tells us of Mrs Ambient only that 'her grief was frantic; she lost her head and said strange things'. The narrator 'imagines' that Miss Ambient's retirement to a convent was because of a guilty conscience, and tells us that his own feels 'compunction', as well it might, for his interference between husband and wife. There is no doubt that Mrs Ambient is responsible for the child's death, but considerable doubt whether we are to accept her sister-in-law's assumption that she de-liberately let him die to save him from being perverted by his father: that it was a 'ferocious' act, and not the result of the unhappy woman's distraction 'sitting there in the sick-chamber in the still hours of the night . . . turning over those pages of genius and wrestling with their magical influence'.

The most striking of Edel's psychological theories is that in the sequence of novels that James wrote after the disaster of *Guy Domville* he was, under the guise of a sequence of child and girl heroines, reliving his own childhood and youth, writing 'an extensive personal allegory of the growing up of Henry James', and that in this strange exercise he was performing an 'imaginative self-therapy' (ii. 292, 294). Edel regards this process as restoring James's 'functional power' and more important his 'creative power'. He could then 'move forward into new depths of adult experience'. It is one of the dangers of a chronological approach to a writer's works that they are seen less as what they are in themselves than as leading on to something else, as if development and progress were synonyms. To many people the novels of this period show James at the very height of his creative powers as an artist. Edel heads this section of his biography 'The Black Abyss'. But the impression we gain from the *Notebooks* is very different. It is of a tremendous surge of creative energy, a feeling of having returned to his true field of action. The disastrous first night of *Guy Domville* was on 5 January 1895. On 12 January James is noting down the anecdote out of which he made *The Turn of the Screw*. On 23 January he writes: 'I take up my *own* old pen again—the pen of all my old unforgettable efforts and sacred struggles. To myself—today—I need say no more. Large and full and high the future still opens. It is now indeed that I may do the work of my life. And I will. x x x x x I have only to *face* my problems.' On 14 February he is writing: 'I have my head, thank God, full of visions. One has never too many—one has never enough.' Ideas for stories and novels pour out, some to be developed, some put aside for a while, some to die. He goes back to consider earlier subjects written down before his incursion into the theatre. On 13 May he has looked back to a story he had been told of a widowed mother refusing to give up her house to her son, and by 11 August he has 'hammered out some 70 pp. of MS'. By December of the same year he has promised Harland for *The Yellow Book* a story 'a 10,000 (a *real* 10,000)' and has begun on 'the little subject of the child, the little girl, whose parents are divorced'. He begins to scheme it out. The extraordinary burst of creative activity in 1895 stems from the great discovery James records in the long note of 14 February, in which he writes that his head is 'full of visions': his discovery of the meaning of 'past bitterness, of recent bitterness'. The last five years spent in writing plays had not been wasted for he had learnt 'the precious lesson, taught me in that roundabout and devious, that cruelly expensive, way, *of the singular value for a narrative plan too* of the (I don't know *what* adequately to call it) divine principle of the Scenario'. It was the discovery of the new method that made James note down with excitement possible subjects on which to employ it. This buoyancy and sense of mastery can be felt in *The Spoils of Poynton*, with its exuberantly comic opening at Waterbath, and in the convolutions of the plot of *What Maisie Knew*. If James at times seems swamped by his material in *The Bostonians*, *The Princess Casamassima*, and *The Tragic Muse*, here he is its master, in full control of his invention. The sequence of novels written in the four years following the collapse of James's theatrical ambitions, *The Spoils of Poynton*, *What Maisie Knew*, *In the Cage*, *The Turn of the Screw*, and *The Awkward Age*, do not give the impression of a man obsessively concerned with personal neuroses, but of a writer immensely curious and observant, one who, like Browning's poet, takes 'cognisance of men and things' with sympathy and humour, exploring a 'recognisable human scene', which is 'transformed through fiction into the predicaments and incapacities of us all'. I am quoting from Dr Kenneth Graham's introduction to his book *Henry James : The Drama of Fulfilment* (1975), a sensitive and subtle study of 'the actual experience of reading' some of James's novels and stories, which stresses 'the representational, moral and emotional qualities', concentrating on 'the fictional scene, its imaginative correspondence with our life, and the dramatic methods by which it is created'.

I hope these comments on Professor Edel's psychological interpretations of James's fictions will not be taken as in any way detracting from what he has so brilliantly given us in his *Life of Henry James*: an absorbing narrative of James's encounter with the world, with so many and such varied worlds, and with so many striking and different personalities. He handles a huge cast of characters with consummate skill. His book is richly revelatory of now vanished social scenes, as well as of James moving among them, with his curious mixture of involvement and non-involvement, in his own search for fulfilment. It is informed throughout by a fine sense of place and time, and warmed by a profound, unsentimental affection and sympathy for James.

This last quality can hardly be said to inform Dr Gittings's *The Older Hardy*, the sequel to his *The Young Thomas Hardy*, which he published in 1975. This was highly, and in my view justly, praised at the time of its appearance for its wealth of information about Hardy's family, its sympathetic account of Hardy's struggles to educate himself, his friendship with the tragic figure of Horace Moule, his orthodoxy as a young man, 'brought up in High Church principles', the sequence of young women who stirred his ever-susceptible heart, including a series of his cousins, and the overwhelming experience of his journey to Cornwall and his meeting with the vigorous, vital Emma Gifford, the first woman of a different social class who had been attracted by him. The chapter in which Dr Gittings outlined the 'grave elements of self-deception in the sympathetic magic of their first association' is admirably balanced. He could not foresee that her energy 'would lead her to bully and domineer in her later years, nor she imagine the huge intellectual gulf that would widen between them'. The book closed with Hardy and Emma at Sturminster, where he wrote *The Return of the Native*. A brief last chapter, 'Old and Young', added a kind of coda, which suggested that the biography was not going to be carried further. In fact, it supplied the 'life-myth' on which Dr Gittings founds the sequel, *The Older Hardy*, published in 1978: that Hardy's 'uprooting from the past' did 'violence to his essential being' (*Early Life*, revised Penguin edition, 1978, p. 298). Dr Gittings presents with the ardour and the repetitiveness of a prosecuting counsel a case against Hardy as a human being. This culminates in his quoting a phrase from a letter of a friend, from whom he had been alienated, as the final verdict on Thomas Hardy: 'There was no largeness of soul' (211 and 173).

The main charge brought against Hardy is his concealment of his family's lowly origins: 'He never breathed to anyone, for instance, that his mother was one of seven children brought up on parish charity; that close relatives, like his uncle John Hardy, were labourers; that several were disreputable or drunk; that his mother, and both his grandmothers, had been pregnant well before their marriages; and that the women in his family, with few exceptions, were domestic servants' (178). Hardy was born in 1840. He was a Victorian, living long before the age when, by an inverted snobbery, it became fashionable to boast of one's lowly origins and of any disgraces that had befallen one's relatives, the more disreputable the better. Dr Gittings, as a historian, must know that it was far from exceptional in rural areas all over Europe for brides to go pregnant to the altar. He comments on the beautiful little poem 'A Church Romance', in which Hardy 'idealized' his own mother and father, that its 'line about their meeting, "Thus their hearts' bond began, in due time signed", begs the questionable fact that their bond of marriage was certainly not signed until it was considerably overdue, when baby Hardy was already four months on the way' (134). Should Hardy not have 'idealized' his parents' happy marriage? Or should he have appended a note, regretting they had delayed the ceremony, as many of their neighbours did? Dr Gittings owns that 'it is easy to condemn Hardy for snobbery, both intellectual and social'; but he immediately withdraws this concession by adding: 'He was certainly more culpable here than his first wife, who has always been blamed for such tendencies; it was, after all, he and not she who inserted into his entry in *Who's Who* the information, unique in that publication, that his wife was the niece of an archdeacon.' (179) It is, after all, perfectly possible that Emma herself asked her husband so to describe her. She had every right to be proud of her distinguished uncle. Although a mere archdeacon, he merited a substantial entry in the *Dictionary of National Biography* as a scholar. But even if this were not so, it seems a small point on which to declare Hardy more culpable than his wife. The larger part of her *Some Recollections* is taken up by establishing what a cultivated, professional family she came from; and Dr Gittings provides evidence of her father's contempt for Hardy as 'a base churl' and of Emma's contempt for his 'peasant origins' (67). That Hardy was highly sensitive to any hint of contempt at his social and educational origins was surely natural. One has only to remember the cruel jibe with which Chesterton summed up his achievement as a novelist in his *Victorian Age in Literature* in 1913, dismissing him as 'a sort of village atheist brooding and blaspheming over the village idiot'. This snobbery finds a curious echo in Dr Gittings's own constant use of the word 'peasant' as a derogatory term. He speaks continually of Hardy's 'peasant morbidity' and his 'peasant meanness' and his 'peasant unwilling-ness to undergo surgery'. He is also fond of using the term 'obsession', speaking of Hardy's obsession with money and his 'ruling obsession about the critics'. While some who have known poverty in youth and become rich in later life enjoy spending money freely and are prodigal, there are others, feeling with Madame Mère 'pourvu que ça dure', who remain cautious and parsimonious; and the cruelty with which Hardy had been treated over his last two novels was surely enough to scar the least sensitive author.

I am not pleading for a curtain to be drawn over the weakness, follies, and sins of writers. I think Professor Crews was right, speaking of Conrad in *Out of My System* (1975), to 'suspect that a certain iconoclasm toward the beauty of artists' lives may be conducive to an honest respect for their art' (46). My objection to *The Older Hardy* is the consistently censorious tone the author adopts and the consistently hostile interpretation he places on the facts. How can he speak of Hardy cutting himself off from his native roots? It is a phrase one could have used if he had transferred himself to London and been content with occasional visits to his family. Instead he settled in Dorchester and remained devoted to his father and mother and to his sister Mary, as well as being, as Dr Gittings tells us, 'genuinely fond' of his younger brother and sister, Henry and Kate. He had to reconcile his profound affection for his family with his wife's lack of sympathy for them, which turned to hostility, and with the fact that intellectually he had outgrown them. His deep feeling for his native county, and for his own and its past, for all he had heard and learnt as a child, was the main source of his imaginative life, but, like every writer, he needed the intellectual stimulus of intercourse with other writers and men of letters, and with friends with whom his family had nothing in common. He had to 'seek the company of the educated', while remaining true to his feeling for the goodness and wisdom that are in the simple. Of course there were great stresses and strains in such a situation. Again, while the health of Emma and Florence is treated sympathetically, Hardy is accused of 'crushing hypochondria', though a long list of painful and disabling ailments could be compiled from the narrative, beginning, soon after his first marriage, with acute inflammation of the bladder, which recurred from time to time. He also suffered from arthritis, particularly in his hands, which is both painful and disabling for a writer, and from constant eye-trouble. There are many references to his frail and exhausted appearance in later life, with particular reference to his hands. Any concession to Hardy, on account of ill health, Dr Gittings quickly withdraws, as when he writes 'Some of this may be explained, though hardly excused, by the fact that . . . Hardy had a recurrence of his chronic bladder trouble' (188).

The most painful aspect of the book is the treatment of Hardy's two marriages. Few authors are easy to live with, because of the absorbing nature of their work. Dr Gittings complains that during the time at Sturminster Hardy 'paid little attention to laying any sort of foundation for a real and mutually satisfying marriage. He was wedded to the overwhelming idea of himself as an author and seeker for truth' (12). This, again, seems to me to reveal a totally unhistoric view. It applies the modern idiom of marriage counselling, and marriage guidance, and endless books and articles on marital problems. Hardy was under the compulsion of a writer, driven by his own genius. He also had to make a living by his pen. And Victorians did not enter upon marriage with the idea that it presented a problem. Dr Gittings reminds us that this was 'the heyday of the idea, now healthily almost defunct, that a wife should devote herself to serving a great artist or writer' (159), but he makes clear that both Emma and Florence seem at the beginning to have accepted such a role. The period at

Sturminster, twenty months, was an idyll, but Hardy was driven by the necessities of his art, something more important than 'a career', to seek for intellectual stimulus, to find a foothold in the literary world of London, and for a while he settled there. After a time Emma was lonely, as Hardy entered what was then primarily a masculine world. But Hardy, although he needed London, had no roots there, and so he took Emma with him to Dorchester. Perhaps the marriage would have fared better if he had not done so. Who knows? It is obvious that, in the end, Hardy and Emma lived virtually separate lives, although living in the same house, only meeting for dinner, although she went with him to London and appearances were kept up. And then, at the age of sixty-seven, what Dr Gittings calls his 'roving eye' fell on Florence Dugdale, forty years his junior, and he was deeply shaken by 'throbbings of noontide'. Today of course, 'those strange laws' by which 'That which mattered most could not be' have been much relaxed; but to Hardy, in the first decade of this century, the notion of leaving his wife was unthinkable, and I am not prepared to regard the deceptions he practised as more reprehensible than what would be regarded as the obvious solution to the problem today. I see Hardy as one who lived under almost intolerable stresses and strains and demands, and I can see interpretations of the facts that Dr Gittings has established that would not lead me to the conclusion that the author of *The Mayor of Casterbridge* and of the poems collected under the epigraph *Veteris vestigia flammae* had 'no largeness of soul'. Dr Gittings sees the poems that Hardy wrote about Emma after her death as given their intensity by a guilt 'more frightful and deep than he dared to describe in these poems'. Edmund Blunden, in the brief study of Hardy he wrote for the English Men of Letters series in 1941, discerned in them 'a voice of self-punishment, of realization that the writer had failed in some questions of approach and contact; but there was the larger feeling that conditions of our existence had been more powerful in the history of that married life than the personal attitude or quality on either side' (137). This seems to me a true judgement. After his wife's death Hardy found that she had left behind her not only *Some Recollections*, which brought back to his memory with unbearable poignancy the magical days of their first meeting and his wooing of her, but also twenty years of diary entries, 'supposedly called "What I think of my Husband"', which Florence Dugdale described as 'those diabolical diaries' (151). In this all Emma's bitterness would seem to have found a vent. Dr Gittings himself refers to her as a 'scourge of husbands' (130). Yet he only notes one poem, 'She

Charged Me', in which 'Emma's bullying manner' appears. There are, perhaps, a few others, such as 'I thought my Heart' in which the speaker refers to the wounds a woman gave. Otherwise, there is regret for a mutual failure:

> Why, then, latterly did we not speak
> Did we not think of those days long dead,
> And ere your vanishing strive to seek
> That time's renewal? We might have said,
> > 'In this bright spring weather
> > We'll visit together
> Those places that once we visited.'

But far more often the remorse and the blame is all Hardy's own and Emma appears as the girl he first knew, and as a loving ghost haunting him and the house they had lived together in.

Dr Gittings says that 'Hardy, for all the tortuous deceptions of his outward life, was seldom anything but honest in poetry. Stress of poetic utterance forced the truth from him' (190). He is writing to introduce the poem that Hardy put last in *Late Lyrics and Earlier*, the moving confessional poem 'Surview', on the text 'Cogitavi vias meas', which begins:

> A cry from the green-grained sticks of the fire
> Made me gaze where it seemed to be:
> 'Twas my own voice talking therefrom to me
> On how I had walked when my sun was higher—
> > My heart in its arrogancy.

But the whole gist of his treatment of the poems Hardy wrote immediately after his wife's death is that in them he concealed the real truth, because 'his full guilt was too horrible to face' and that he 'underlined with continual guilty insistence the suddenness and unexpectedness of her death' (153). This interpretation rests on the two powerful and painful paragraphs in which he describes the last two days of Emma's life (149–50). I wish I knew whose memories, or what documents, these paragraphs are drawing on, for, contrary to his usual practice, Dr Gittings gives no reference here. And I should like to have been told the date of Hardy's letter to Mrs Henniker, in which Hardy wrote to this close and much loved friend 'Emma's death was absolutely unexpected by me, the doctor, and anybody', adding 'I have reproached myself for not having guessed there might be some internal mischief at work.' Dr Gittings tells us that it was 'at the time', but I should like to know how soon after the shock of being called upstairs to find his wife *in extremis* we are to believe that Hardy invented this story. As for the alteration Hardy made when he altered for publication in *Late Lyrics* the early draft of the poem 'Best Times', I would like to point out that the revision makes the last verse chime with the others, which are all concerned with moments of happiness that, at the time, the poet did not realize would not come again. Poets are 'not on oath', and the first draft, although truer to fact in the detail of Emma's 'climbing the stair' after 'a languid rising', conflicts with the title 'Best Times' and with the whole point of the poem. And it is not true that Hardy had concealed in his poetry his wife's failing health. 'The Walk' was published among the lyrics of the collection headed *Veteris vestigia flammae* :

> You did not walk with me
> Of late to the hill-top tree
>> By the gated ways,
>> As in earlier days;
>> You were weak and lame,
>> So you never came.
> And I went alone, and I did not mind,
>> Not thinking of you as left behind.

As with Professor Edel, so I must add here that my complaints about the tone of *The Older Hardy*, and the hostility of the interpretation of the facts of Hardy's life, do not diminish my admiration for the amount of information Dr Gittings has brought to light.

I have, perhaps unfairly, concentrated on two recent biographies to express the disquiet I feel at the high claims being made for modern literary biography. It is rather ironic that when in 1927 Virginia Woolf declared that, compared with his Victorian predecessors, the biographer of the twentieth century had 'become an artist', one reason she gave was the 'dimunition in size' of modern biographies. The availability of materials, and the freedom from all those inhibitions that made Johnson give it as his rule that, when '*walking upon ashes under which the fire is not yet extinguished . . . it will be proper rather to say nothing that is false, than all that is true*', has produced biographies of recently dead writers that more than rival the Victorian in size. When twelve years later she had changed her mind and reduced the biographer from an artist to a craftsman, she unkindly pointed to the 'high death rate' of biographies compared with poetry and fiction. Surely this is true. At least in my own experience I can say that with some great exceptions—the most obvious one is Boswell's *Life of Johnson*—a literary biography, once read, I use as a work of reference, an invaluable one, but not something to reread. The same applies for me to most works of literary criticism. I do not read them for their own sake, and rarely re-read them. I make grateful use of them, again, as works of reference.

Professor Ellmann, in his inaugural lecture at Oxford on *Literary Biography*, reprinted in *Golden Codgers* (1973), wisely warned us that 'we cannot know completely the intricacies with which any mind negotiates with its surroundings to produce literature. The controlled seething out of which great works come is not likely to yield all its secrets.' Yet when he goes on to say that the biographer's effort is 'to know another person who has lived as well as we know a character in fiction, and better than we know ourselves', I demur. What we know from a biography is an enormous amount *about* a person who has lived, facts of his life, the views of his friends and contemporaries, in fact, all what we call research can discover; and we know the biographer's interpretation of the material he has gathered. This is different from the way we know a character in fiction. We know him by his actions, by what he does, and even more by what he says, how he behaves to others and others to him, what they say about him and what he in return says about them. The author may or may not comment on his characters, but the more the author comments, the more he 'places' them for our approval or disapproval, the less vividly they live in our imaginations. We can discuss, and disagree over, the characters in a great play or a great novel as we can discuss and disagree over the characters of friends and acquaintances, whom we also know by their actions and their speech while being deeply ignorant of many things about them. With living persons and with characters of fiction our imaginations are at work, and in both cases we can be surprised and have to accommodate unexpectedness. We respond in something of the same way to letters and memoirs, and I find I also respond to biographies of historical characters, particularly obscure ones, where I learn of their 'deeds and words' and am not led into speculations about their inner lives.

I hope I shall not be thought of as speaking to a Research Association in denigration of biographical research. I believe with Eliot that a fact has more value than an opinion and that even the discovery of Shakespeare's laundry lists might prove useful to someone some day. Look what Mrs Langley Moore made out of the accounts of Byron's Italian Secretary. What I question is the claim that the unfettered freedom of the modern literary biographer makes him any more able to arrive at the 'real man' and his 'inner life' than his more ignorant and reticent predecessors were, and what I dislike is the subordination of his subject's true achievement to the enquiry into his psyche, or the disregard of it in telling us what he was really like. Dr Gittings asserts that 'the last fifty years have been a golden age of biography'; but Mr A. O. J. Cockshut, in his essays on Victorian Biography, *Truth to Life*, attempted to demonstrate that for nearly two hundred years we have been living in a golden age of biographical writings. He was not concerned with strictly literary biographies, but he put his finger on what I think is the one necessity of a good biography: that its author remains aware of the 'mystery of human personality' and that he preserves 'a salutary humility . . . in the august presence of another soul'.

Index